Philosophy of Brahman

Philosophy of Brahman

A. Ramamurty

D.K. Printworld (P) Ltd.
Publishers of Indian Traditions

Cataloging in Publication Data — DK
[Courtesy: D.K. Agencies (P) Ltd. <docinfo@dkagencies.com>]

Ramamurty A. (Aryasomayajula), 1935-
Philosophy Brahman / A. Ramamurty.
p. cm.
Includes bibliographical references (p).
ISBN 13: 9788124605530
ISBN 10: 812460553X
1. Hindu philosophy. 2. Brahman. I. Title.

DDC 181.4 22

First published in India, 2010
ISBN 13: 978-81-246-0553-0 ISBN 10: 81-246-0553-X

Published and printed by:
D.K. Printworld (P) Ltd.
Regd. office : *'Srikunj,'* F-52, Bali Nagar
Ramesh Nagar Metro Station
New Delhi – 110 015
Phones : (011) 2545 3975; 2546 6019; *Fax* : (011) 2546 5926
E-mail: indology@dkprintworld.com
Web: www.dkprintworld.com

Preface

THIS book is in one sense a critique of metaphysics usually viewed as an attempt to explain the existence of the world in terms of a reality which is regarded as the ultimate cause or source of the world, and in another sense to understand metaphysics as a profoundly significant attempt to know or understand the true or real nature of what is there or what we all experience empirically, or the world. With the exception of Nāgārjuna and Śaṅkara, the philosophers belonging to different schools of philosophy tried to understand the world in terms of a reality which is supposed to be the explanation of it. In that they all have taken for granted that the world has no independent existence or cannot exist by itself, and the nature of the world is what it is known empirically. Thus without trying to understand whether the world requires any explanation for its existence, either metaphysical or theological, they tried to find a metaphysical explanation for its existence in terms of a reality which is other than the world. However, in the other approach to metaphysics which we discern in the philosophy of Śaṅkara which is in tune with the basic insights of the Upaniṣads, a comprehensive attempt is made to know or understand the true or real nature of what we know empirically, or the world before any attempt is made to explain its existence. This kind of approach to metaphysics in which the object is not to find a causal explanation for the existence of the world but to know or understand its nature is free from the various formidable problems which are inevitable in the other kind of metaphysics.

We tried to analyse and understand critically the basic concepts involved in the ontological problem of *Brahman*, like the nature of the world, its causal explanation, nature and ontological status of matter, consciousness and its relation to spirit or self with a view to understanding the Advaitic insight that *Brahman* is the true nature of what we experience and know empirically. As the true or real nature of the world of empirical experience, *Brahman* is not a reality which is other than the reality of the world, and if the world is known in its true or real nature we may realize that the world and *Brahman* are not really different. A philosophical analysis of the world of empirical experience may give rise to the idea that there are no two things of world and *Brahman*, or matter and spirit ultimately. We thus tried to understand the Advaitic position by way of understanding the meaning of the world. Matter and spirit constitute the world of empirical experience, while *Brahman* is seen or known as pure consciousness. Therefore we have tried to analyse and understand the nature and reality of matter, and its relation to consciousness which is very crucial in understanding the nature of *Brahman*, as well as the significance of Advaita.

I take this opportunity to thank sincerely Shri Susheel K. Mittal, director, D.K. Printworld (P) Ltd., New Delhi for his service through publications to project all that is noble and significant in Indian heritage and culture, including Indian philosophy and religion.

Hyderabad, **A. Ramamurty**
21 June 2010

Contents

Introduction

In the history of Indian philosophy those who had seriously questioned the possibility of metaphysics was the Buddha, and the different schools of Buddhism inspired by the teachings of the Buddha. Any enquiry into the problems of metaphysics, like the nature of the world, the reason for its existence, the nature and existence of ultimate reality, the nature and destiny of man, is futile as there can be no clear and definite solution to the problems, and more importantly, the metaphysical problems have no relevance or significance to man, and his existential concerns. Instead of trying to understand the problems of metaphysics or ontology which have no significance in understanding the practical problems of man, philosophy should concern itself to understand and solve some of the practical or existential problems of man like suffering. However, if we try to know why philosophy should turn its attention to understanding practical problems of man, like suffering, but not to the theoretical problems like the nature of the world, the reason for its existence, the existence and nature of what is ultimately real, we find no convincing reasons, or sufficient justification in favour of practical approach. Moreover, who can decide what is practically significant to man? The philosophers who belong to the school of Pūrva-Mīmāṁsā also deny the possibility of metaphysics, as according to them, metaphysical understanding of transcendental problems will have no objective validity, though it is meaningful to the extent it can help or encourage man to follow the path of righteousness as prescribed in the Veda. The materialist philosophers (Cārvākas) are the first to question the possibility of metaphysics on epistemological grounds. However, these philosophers have tried to give reasons or justify their positions in denying the possibility of metaphysics. Though each system or school of philosophy has its own reasons for denying the possibility of metaphysics, broadly speaking the justification for denying the possibility of metaphysics is twofold. While some have denied the possibility of metaphysics on epistemological grounds, or in terms of man's ability to know anything beyond the world of empirical experience, others consider metaphysics as a futile exercise because they doubt the utility of metaphysics or its significance to man, and his problems.

Most of the philosophers of Vedānta have tried to develop or construct their systems of metaphysics on the basis of the Upaniṣads as, according to them, the authority of the Upaniṣads, is sufficient to justify metaphysics. The fundamental problem of metaphysics, with which the Upaniṣads are concerned, is the existence and nature of *Brahman*, the explanation for the existence of the world. Therefore, the main concern of most of the Vedāntins is to develop a philosophy of *Brahman* based on the Upaniṣads. However, after realizing that no systematic and consistent philosophy of the Upaniṣads, or a logically coherent doctrine of *Brahman* cannot be developed on the basis of the Upaniṣads most of them have resorted to reasoning either to defend or justify their positions or in criticizing and demolishing the positions of others. Their main concern in invoking reason is not to find justification for the testimony of the Upaniṣads, but to criticize and destroy the claims of their opponents, as well as to reconcile and systematize the Upaniṣadic statements or ideas. However, they have not tried to understand how the Upaniṣads can provide or offer us knowledge about the transcendental realities, like *Brahman*. They have not tried to understand and explain in what way the Upaniṣads are better equipped to know *Brahman*, or what is the justification for us to accept the authority of the Upaniṣads in transcendental matters. They accepted the authority of the Upaniṣads as final in transcendental matters, like *Brahman*, which is, however, contrary to the spirit of the Upaniṣads. The important thing which they wanted to achieve by accepting the authority of the Upaniṣads in understanding the metaphysical problems, like the existence and nature of *Brahman*, is to arrive at knowledge that is definite and beyond doubt which they think cannot be achieved in terms of rational understanding of man, as it is evident from the fact that there are as many systems of metaphysics as there are philosophers, and each system is in conflict with the other systems. However, the systems of Vedānta developed by the interpreters of Vedānta are equally in conflict with each other, and we find as many systems of Vedānta metaphysics as there are interpreters of Vedānta. And most of the systems of Vedānta are theological in nature, as each interpretation of Vedānta has given birth to a religious sect, or is associated with an existing religious sect, as most of the interpreters tried to provide scriptural basis or justification for some of the religious sects, and their beliefs. However, we have to admit that the nature of the metaphysical problems is such that philosophers cannot provide any definite solutions to them, but does not, however, diminish the value of metaphysics as a philosophical activity, if we understand the object or meaning of metaphysics differently.

The main concern of most of the philosophers belonging to different systems of philosophy developed in India is to find a causal explanation for the existence of the world. They tried to know or understand the reality that is supposed to be the cause of the world of empirical experience, or the main concern of metaphysics, according to them, is to find causal explanation for the existence of the world. And in almost all such attempts the purpose of knowing or understanding the cause of the world is to help man in understanding the nature of his destiny, as each system of philosophy has tried to understand the destiny of man in terms of its understanding of the cause of the world, and its nature. It is not, however, the case that the philosophers first conceived the destiny of man, and then tried to project the nature of ultimately reality accordingly. Even the materialist philosophers have not tried to justify sensual form of life in terms of their metaphysics. As, according to their philosophical investigation, the ultimate reality is known to be matter and the destiny of man will be to enjoy life in this world as the idea of something in man surviving the death is inconsistent with its ontological position. The Sāṁkhya philosophers, who are least influenced by the Indian scriptures, tried to understand the destiny of man in tune with its dualistic metaphysics. However, our concern here is not to find logical fallacies in different systems of metaphysics, but to understand the basic presupposition which is common to most of the philosophers as far as their understanding of the meaning and object of metaphysics is concerned.

Each system of philosophy has developed its system of metaphysics based on its understanding of the world and its nature. And what is common to most of the systems of metaphysics, developed in India, is the presupposition that the world of empirical experience has no independent existence, or is a caused reality. Therefore, the object of metaphysics is to know or understand the reality that is the cause of the world, or to provide an explanation for the existence of the world in terms of its cause, and most of the systems tried to understand the problem in terms of rational understanding though they acknowledge the authority of scriptures. But one thing they all have taken for granted is that the world is what is known through empirical experience, and the only thing that is to be known about the world is its origin, or the reason for its existence, as without understanding the cause of the world our understanding of the world will not be complete and perfect. However, most of the philosophers are not clear in what sense the world exists. Does it refer to an entity which we can know and understand? Is it a fact among other facts which needs explanation for its existence? But most of the Indian philosophers are aware that the world means the totality of facts which we experience, or the facts of empirical experience constitute the world, and therefore the world as such is not real, or has no existence. Therefore, to explain the existence of the world really means to understand the reason or reasons for the existence of facts which are the objects of empirical experience. We have to know or understand whether one and the same reality can be the explanation of all the facts that constitute the world, or whether we can explain the existence of all the facts in terms of a single substance or reality. But as the things and phenomena that constitute the world are so varied in their natures it is not meaningful to explain their existence in terms of a single substance or reality. All the objects of gold can find their explanation in gold, but gold cannot explain the existence of things made of clay. This led the Vaiśeṣika philosophers to think in terms of several realities to explain the existence of the world, or the multiplicity of facts. However, it is the Sāṁkhya philosophers who are the first to see the possibility of explaining the existence of the world in terms of two realities of matter or nature (*prakṛti*) and spirit (*puruṣa*). Their realization that nature or matter is blind, or is devoid of the light of consciousness, the source of knowledge, and spirit is lame or is not dynamic to explain the movement in the world is a very significant step in understanding the world as well as in providing a plausible explanation for its existence. The world of facts can be subsumed under the categories of matter and spirit, or these two realities are sufficient to understand and explain the world of facts. But the matter and spirit cannot be explained in terms of a single reality for the reason that matter and spirit are opposed to each other. This realization seems to be the stumbling block for all philosophers in their efforts to explain the existence of the world in terms of a single reality. Matter and spirit cannot be the explanation of each other because of the oppositions between them, and for the same reason one and the same reality cannot be the explanation of their existence. This problem is faced by all the philosophers, and their philosophical arguments or reasons to overcome the problem of opposition between matter and spirit are full of logical fallacies. This is also the problem faced by almost all the Vedāntins. In modern times, Sri Aurobindo was the first to realize the importance of the problem, and in his own way tried to reconcile matter and spirit in order to provide a more meaningful or adequate explanation for the existence of the world. He might have been influenced in his attempts to reconcile matter and spirit by the modern theory of evolution, and the Tāntric tradition of India. In the Tāntric tradition, the nature of consciousness and its relation to matter are conceived differently. The problem was felt by Śrī Rāmānuja also who in his own manner tried to reconcile matter and spirit by conceiving them as forming the body and self of *Brahman*.

The basic presupposition in all attempts to explain the existence of the world either in terms of a single reality, or in terms of several realities is that the world cannot exist by itself, or has no independent existence. Thus the main concern of metaphysics, according to most of the systems of Indian philosophy, is to find a causal explanation for the existence of the world. The Sāṁkhya philosophy whose understanding of matter is so comprehensive, rich and beautiful we do not come across such an understanding of matter in other systems. However, most of the Vedāntins have accepted the Sāṁkhya view or understanding of matter. Matter, according to Sāṁkhya, is the source of tender emotions in man. It can entice man, and also help him in liberating himself from the enticement. All the creations of man like music, literature, philosophy, etc. are the creations or expressions of mind, a subtle form of matter, and mind in its subtlety is like spirit or consciousness so as to be able to reflect the nature of spirit in itself. However, they have not gone further in exploring or understanding more deeply the nature of matter before reaching the conclusion that it is fundamentally different from consciousness or spirit. Here we have to point out that our understanding of matter has not remained the same throughout. The Sāṁkhya conception of matter is different from that of the

Cārvākas, and other realist philosophers. The nature or meaning of causation also differs in relation to the reality that is regarded as the cause of the world. The nature or meaning of causation in relation to a material reality or substance will be different from the nature or meaning of causation in relation to a spiritual reality. For instance, the manner in which gold and the objects made of gold are related is fundamentally different from the manner in which mind and its creations or expressions are related. In the case of mind and its expressions we cannot say that the mind is the cause, and its various creations or expressions are the effect, as we can say of gold and the objects of gold. The mind and its expressions are not related in the usual sense as they are not different because we do not know what mind is without its expressions, and at the same time we cannot say that the expressions are the mind. Mind is more than its expressions as its existence is not exhausted by the expressions, and expressions cannot have existence without mind.

We find in Indian philosophy another approach to metaphysics which is basically different from the one in which the main concern is to find causal explanation for the existence of the world. In the classical Advaita causation has no place either in understanding *Brahman* or in understanding its relation to the world, as they are not seen as two different realities. The basic concern of metaphysics, according to Advaita, is not to explain the existence of the world of empirical experience, but to know or understand its real or true nature. Before we try to explain the existence of the world in terms of *Brahman* if we analyse and understand the various concepts involved in the metaphysical problem of *Brahman* like the world, matter, spirit, causation and *Brahman* we come to realize how the concern of metaphysics to explain the existence of the world is meaningless as the world of empirical experience is not a caused or dependent reality. It is in its true nature not different from *Brahman*, the supposed cause of itself. And because of the realization of non-difference between *Brahman* and the world so many problems of metaphysics, which are formidable otherwise, get themselves dissolved. When we come to know or realize that what we know about the world empirically is not the real or true nature of it then we start doubting whether the metaphysics based on the empirical experience of the world can really be meaningful and valid. As the law of causation is significant in understanding the facts of the world, or the world of empirical experience, we accept its importance in understanding the world also. What is significant in understanding the facts of the world may not be significant in understanding the world as such as we do not know whether a law that is valid in relation to the facts of the world can also be valid in relation to the world or the totality of facts. However, many philosophers in their attempts to understand the world have tried to extend the law of causation to the world as well as to the reality, the supposed cause or explanation of the world, which is not part of the empirical world.

We think we know a reality because we are able to define it, and that is the case with matter and spirit. If we do not take into consideration all the facts about a thing or reality, especially when it is dynamic in its nature, our definition of it will not be comprehensive and valid. We think of matter as something static, dull, and governed by mechanical laws as we are guided in our understanding of matter by certain facts we observe in the world like rocks and metals. And in relation to spirit which is seen as noble, good and creative, we understand matter as evil, mechanical, and as that which hampers the growth or development of spirit, and its fulfilment. On the other hand, if we understand by matter all that is an object of knowledge or experience, then our understanding of matter will be significantly different from its popular conception in which it is regarded as the source of all that is negative and evil. According to the philosophers of Vedānta and Sāṁkhya, which is shared by most of the Indian philosophers, matter comprehends the whole world, except the fact of consciousness, or the world with the exception of spirit or consciousness is a manifestation of matter. Human mind and all its creations, which form a very significant aspect of the world, are subtle forms of matter. Matter is much more than what we popularly think about it in which we limit our understanding of matter to certain facts which fit into the popular definition of matter. But there is development in our understanding of matter. Now, we know or understand that light, beauty of a flower, serenity of nature, creativity of mind, tender emotions like love, and at the same the destructive capacity of an atom bomb, and other calamities of nature are the forms of manifestation of matter. In its subtle form as mind, matter is as transparent as spirit, and its creations like music and literature are regarded as spiritual, though in reality they are physical in nature; sound is physical. Therefore, the Advaitins see in mind the likeness of spirit because of which there is confusion between mind and spirit. However, this is meaningful only at the level of understanding *Brahman* in which we negate or deny so many things in order to know the essence or essential reality of *Brahman*.

Similarly, our conception of consciousness or spirit, based on our empirical experience, may not be true to its real nature. We see opposition between spirit and matter as at the level of empirical experience the spirit is fundamentally different from matter. And if we think that the world of empirical experience is a manifestation of matter the spirit does not belong to the world. But the conception of self or spirit as we find it in the basic texts of Vedānta or the Upaniṣads is different from the other conceptions of self. In the Upaniṣads, *Brahman* is seen as the essence (*ātman*) of all that is there, but not only of man. The ultimate reality or *Brahman* is known in relation to the world of empirical experience as the essence or the essential reality of all that is there. It is the inner unity of all that is there or the world, or the world is one or a unity because *Brahman* is the reality of all the facts that constitute the world. As the essence of all that is there *Brahman* is the essence (*ātman*) of man also. And man can know the essence or the essential reality of himself directly or without any mediation, and consciousness is identified as the essence or self of man. Therefore, the self or essence (*ātman*) of man is intrinsic to his reality. It is not something different from the reality of man as the self is discovered while understanding the reality of man. The essence of a thing is not extrinsic to the thing. It is intrinsic to the thing as it is that which sustains the thing and gives it its identity. In the *Chāndogya* and *Bṛhadāraṇyaka Upaniṣads*, we find the logic of discovery of *Brahman* stated in clear terms, and with highly significant examples or analogies. In all the analogies or examples given in the *Chāndogya Upaniṣad*, while teaching *Brahman* as the essence of all that is there, it is said that as life sap of a tree pervades the tree, sustains it and forms the unity of the tree, so also *Brahman* pervades all that is there as its essence, and sustains all. Therefore, the world cannot exist and sustain itself without *Brahman*. And in man *Brahman* is known as consciousness which is the self or the essence of man. And it is only in trying to know or understand the essential reality of man or his essence we distinguish what is essential to be a human being from the other aspects of his reality which though belong to man are not significant in understanding the reality of man. Thus the essence of man is distinguished from the other aspects of man, or what is changing in man is distinguished from what is not changing in him, or what is ultimately real in man is distinguished from what is real in him to understand and identify the reality of man. This does not, however, mean that all other aspects or facts of man are not integral to the reality of man. In asserting that the life or self of a tree is its sap we are not denying the reality of its trunk, roots, branches, etc. as in knowing the tree they are not as significant as the life sap of a tree. It is the life sap that sustains the tree, and is the reason for the unity of the tree. A tree can survive even if some of the branches are cut, but not when its life sap is dried up. And if there is no tree there is no problem of discovering the sap as its essence. In other words, only in relation to the tree the sap is meaningful as its essence. The sap is intrinsic to the tree. It is only in relation to the world of empirical experience *Brahman* is known as the essence as well as the unity of the world, otherwise *Brahman* as the essence and unity of the world will have no meaning. Therefore, in identifying *Brahman* as the essence and unity of the world we are not denying the other aspects of the world, and more importantly, we are not separating *Brahman* from the world or the world from *Brahman*. If *Brahman* is something other than the world then it cannot be the essence of the world, and then we cannot say that knowledge of *Brahman* is significant in knowing the world, or vice versa. It is only in relation to the world of empirical experience we come to know *Brahman*, as both are related, and if they are not related, or if *Brahman* has nothing to do with the reality of the world of empirical experience, or the world has no significance in knowing *Brahman*, then the problem of *Brahman* will have no significance to man.

And if *Brahman* is fundamentally a spiritual reality then the way it can be related to the world of empirical experience cannot be one of causation. We find in the classical tradition of India the relation between *Brahman* and the world compared to breathing in and breathing out in living human beings, or to a creative person (*kavi*) to his creation (*kāvya*). The coming into existence of the world from *Brahman* is as spontaneous as the growth of hair in a living human being, or a web from a spider, or sparks from a burning fire. All these are not cases of causation. A creative person is not the cause of his creations, or the process of breathing is not causally related to man. On the other hand, if we say that *Brahman* is the cause of the world we have to face so many problems. How to conceive the nature of *Brahman* before the world comes into existence? Does it occupy space, and if it occupies space we have to think of space as existing prior to *Brahman*. And if *Brahman* is not a limited reality there can be no space for the world to occupy when it comes into existence? And if *Brahman* is absolutely perfect what must have been the reason for *Brahman* to cause the world to exist? If we attribute any motive to *Brahman* in causing the world to exist we have to compromise with the perfection of *Brahman*. All our understanding of *Brahman* is meaningful only in relation to the world of empirical experience. More importantly, there will be no justification for us to accept the theory of causation of the world when we cannot prove that the world is caused to exist? And if the world is not caused to exist, and *Brahman* is a spiritual reality then we have to think of a completely different relation between *Brahman* and the world as it cannot be one of causation. A creative person and his creations are not related as the creations are spontaneous outburst of creativity (*sṛṣṭi*). A musician and his musical creations are not related as cause and effect. The creations are expressions of creativity for which there is no reason or motive. Creativity expresses itself in various ways and forms, and as the process is not mechanical we cannot determine the nature of creativity, or the forms of its expression. And we cannot also say that creativity, and the forms of its expressions are related because they are not different. We cannot think of creativity without its expression, and though we accept that a creative person is more than his creations he is not different from his creations. While creations depend upon the creative person, the existence of the creative person is not dependent upon the creations. However, it is through the creations we come to know the nature of creativity as they are means of knowing the person and his nature. Thus *Brahman* does not depend upon the world for its existence, but the knowledge of *Brahman* is possible only in and through the world, the creative expression of *Brahman* (*sṛṣṭi*). But the world depends logically for its existence on *Brahman* as without *Brahman* there can be no world. Thus as mentioned in one of the Upaniṣads, *Brahman* is creation (*sṛṣṭi*) as creation is not an act but an expression of *Brahman*.

This way of understanding the world, and its logical dependence upon *Brahman* for its existence is fundamentally different from all other metaphysical theories or explanations in which *Brahman* is regarded as the cause of the world. This type of approach to the world as well as to metaphysics we find in the writings of Nāgārjuna, and later in the works of Śaṅkara. According to them, if we know the real nature of the world we come to realize the non-difference between *Brahman* and the world as *Brahman* is the true nature of the world. They are not really two different realities so that they can be related causally or otherwise. Thus if we try to know or understand the world dispassionately or without giving it a value we can know the true or real nature of the world. On the other hand, if we impose on the world of empirical experience or on matter certain values, which are religious or cultural, we fail to understand the nature of the world objectively or dispassionately. And if we try to understand the nature of matter without any prejudice, and keeping in view the varied forms of its manifestation we can know matter or the world, as much of the world is a manifestation of matter, in its true nature which may be the outward form of spirit. And when we try to understand the logic of discovering the self we come to know that it is known as the essential reality of man, but not as alien to human reality. Self is the essence of man, but not an independent reality living in man, and therefore the spirit or consciousness, and man or his body and mind are integrally related or are one.

Now, can we say that one way of doing metaphysics is more meaningful than the other way of doing metaphysics. When compared to metaphysics as an investigation into the cause of the world, or to find a causal explanation for the existence of the world, metaphysics as an attempt to understand the real or true nature of the world of empirical experience is more meaningful. When we come to know that there are as many theories of the world as there are of *Brahman* and its nature we come to realize that the world is also a problem. When there are several views or theories about the world we cannot say that all of them are true, or there is no problem about the world and its nature. When we find several views which are not consistent with each other about the world there is sufficient justification in trying to know or understand the real or true nature of the world. However, we find competition between metaphysics conceived as an attempt to know the true or real nature of the world, and science which is equally interested in understanding or knowing the world as objectively as possible. Knowing that science is well equipped to know the world because of its method as well as the equipment it has developed can we think that the metaphysical understanding of the world has an advantage over the scientific understanding of the world. Here we have to point out that both science and philosophy depend on certain facts which they consider as significant or crucial in understanding the world. For instance, when one wants to understand matter he chooses or selects certain things, and depends upon them for his understanding as matter is not a homogeneous reality. By studying a piece of gold one can understand gold as gold is a homogeneous reality. Can we say the same thing about the world, or can we find a sample representative of the world to know or understand the world? For example, our understanding of rocks may not be helpful or significant in understanding plants, and our understanding of plants may not help us in understanding animals, and our understanding animals may not help us in understanding human reality, and even our understanding of human reality may not help us in understanding the nature of creativity found in certain human beings. Thus seeing the diversity in nature can we generalize about the world, or take any one sample or example to understand the world? Is there any paradigm that can help us in knowing or understanding the world? Now, understanding matter is one thing, for which a scientist may take a representative sample or example, but to understand matter in relation to spirit is another thing. We cannot say that both are the forms of the same reality, or spirit is a subtle form of matter for which there is no demonstrable evidence. Unless one tries to know or understand matter through the best forms of its manifestation we cannot say our understanding of matter is comprehensive and perfect. Now, what we come to know about matter as manifested in man we cannot know through any of its other manifestations. Man is not only the best form of manifestation of spirit, but also of matter, and at the same time he is the only source to know or understand the nature of relationship between matter and spirit. If we accept that to understand matter we have to take into consideration the best possible form of its manifestation we have to accept the reality of man as the best possible form of matter, and science is not equipped to study man who is a personal being with subjectivity. The method it has developed to study the observable things is not adequate to study a reality which cannot be directly observed though it is real. Man has an inner dimension to his existence or he has subjectivity which is more significant in understanding human reality, and that cannot be studied objectively as it cannot be observed directly by anyone else than the person concerned. The creativity, and the varied forms of its expression cannot also be studied by others, and even for the creative person it is not completely intelligible. It is in a sense a mystery which, however, helps us to know the nature of human reality. Human creativity is not only a mystery for others, but also to the creative person, and the sense of mystery is expressed by saying that it is divine. And if we accept that human reality is the best possible paradigm to understand the world of empirical experience, or in which the reality of the world finds its best possible form of expression or manifestation, we have to study man in depth to know the world of empirical experience. The appeal of religion to man, though he accepts and appreciates science, is because religion reveals something significant about human reality which science cannot do. A scientist *qua* scientist cannot understand human reality, as to understand human reality one has to understand oneself which is possible only by being subjective or by living the internal life. Therefore, human reality is really significant in knowing or understanding the reality of the world, and the science because of its methodological constraints cannot fully comprehend the reality of man as it involves subjectivity or internal life as well as creativity. In the human reality we find the best possible form of matter as well as the true nature of spirit which is creativity, and in man both are one or are united.

Whether metaphysics viewed as an investigation into the reality of the world, or as an attempt to know or understand the world in its real or true nature, but not to find a causal explanation for its existence, can arrive at a definite view or understanding of the world, is not relevant to our purpose. In trying to analyse and understand the concepts involved in the problem of *Brahman* or in trying to find out the true nature of the world man comes to understand or realize himself more fully or perfectly, and his self-knowledge helps him in understanding the origin and validity of the various concepts involved in understanding the world. In and through the philosophical activity in which we analyse the concepts to understand their meaning and validity we are freed from believing or accepting certain ideas or concepts without properly understanding them. For instance, human attitude to matter and spirit as well as the relationship between them, or his understanding of them, are influenced by attitudes and beliefs which he inherits or accepts without understanding their origin and validity. Thus we find so many isms about matter and spirit which man tends to believe, as he is not encouraged to analyse and understand the concepts for himself as if such a thing is beyond his ability or competency. On the other hand, if one can know that there is no mystery involved in understanding the world and its nature he is encouraged to understand for himself the concepts of matter and spirit, and their relationship which gives him real freedom from all kinds of dogmas about himself and the world. This is a significant gain in doing metaphysics for himself. And this is the path of knowledge which everyone has to tread for himself. But in keeping faith in science to know the reality of man as well as that of the world man forgets that there can be no clear and definite knowledge about them as creativity, the real significance of spirituality, is involved in understanding them. In trying to understand the meaning of spirituality or creativity one has to go deep into his inner life. The creativity is not amenable to scientific understanding as it is something which cannot be objectivized. And if creativity or spirituality which is the innermost life of man is to be studied objectively it ceases to be meaningful as then the subjective character of human creativity is lost.

If we accept the significance of human subjectivity or his inner life in understanding the meaning of spirituality or creativity which is not amenable to laws which govern the world of empirical experience, and without knowing it our understanding of the world will be incomplete and superficial, we have to admit the significance and validity of insights which reveal the inner or spiritual or creative life of man, and the Upaniṣads are meaningful as they contain such insights. And as the world depends for its existence on the creativity of *Brahman*, but not on the laws which science can understand, the Upaniṣads are highly significant and valuable in understanding *Brahman*.

This work is an attempt to analyse and understand the concept of *Brahman* which is fundamental to all the schools of Vedānta. And in a broad sense it is also fundamental to Indian philosophy, as the concept of *Brahman* has attracted the attention of almost all the philosophers and thinkers of India. In modern times, both academic and non-academic philosophers have tried to understand the concept of *Brahman* in their own ways. However, no systematic and thoroughly philosophic approach of *Brahman* is to be found in the modern Indian philosophy, as most of the Vedāntins have shown interest in popularizing Vedānta. As a result we find several doctrines of *Brahman* developed mainly to satisfy the needs or requirements of people. Vedānta is mainly conceived as a sort of spiritualism opposed to materialism.

This is an attempt, maybe first of its kind, to develop a philosophy of *Brahman* in which the various concepts involved in understanding *Brahman* are philosophically analysed to understand the problem of *Brahman* in all its aspects. This also helps in understanding Indian life and culture, as the Vedānta has played a significant role in shaping the Indian mind. This work is thoroughly analytical in its approach to *Brahman*. Without the analysis of the concepts involved in the development of the concept of *Brahman*, as well as the context of its origin in the philosophical tradition of India, it is not possible to understand *Brahman* and its nature. In the first two chapters of this work we have tried to discuss the two ways of understanding the world which gave rise to two different conceptions of metaphysics, or two different ways of doing metaphysics. According to one way of understanding the world, the object is to find a causal explanation for the existence of the world of empirical experience as according to this way of understanding the world, the world cannot exist by itself or has no independent existence. Therefore the object or concern of metaphysics is to find a causal explanation for the existence of the world. The different problems involved in understanding the world in terms of *Brahman* conceived as the cause of the world are fully analysed and discussed. In the second chapter, we discussed the other way of understanding the world, the object of which is to know the real or true nature of *Brahman*, because the nature of the world as known to empirical experience may not be its true or real nature, as is evident from the fact that there are as many views or theories of the world as there are views or doctrines of *Brahman*. Therefore an investigation into the true or real nature of what we empirically experience is both legitimate and justified. According to this approach, the object of metaphysics is not to find a causal explanation for the existence of the world but to understand the true or real nature of the world. In the third chapter, the problem of *Brahman* conceived as the reality of the world of empirical experience is discussed. In the fourth chapter we have tried to understand whether matter can be the reality of *Brahman*. We have tried to understand the concept of matter according to Indian philosophical tradition and tried to understand its nature taking into consideration all the forms of its manifestation, including human mind and its creativity. In the chapter on consciousness, we have discussed in what sense consciousness can be the reality of *Brahman*, and if that is the case how to understand the reality of matter and its relation to consciousness. In the chapter on spirit or self we tried to maintain a distinction between consciousness and self or spirit, the essential reality of man. We have tried to understand the logic of its discovery as well as the significance of self in understanding *Brahman*. Thus in the light of our analysis of the various concepts involved in understanding the problem, our understanding of *Brahman* is thorough and comprehensive, and is philosophical.

1

Approach to World I

METAPHYSICS is the dominant concern of almost all the systems of philosophy developed in India, and each system has developed its own system of metaphysics depending upon the way it understands the world and its nature. However, we discern in the philosophical tradition of India two basically different ways of understanding the world. Before we discuss the two ways of understanding the world we have to explain, though briefly, the concept of world, as we find it in the Indian philosophical tradition as our understanding of the world depends upon what we mean by it. What do the Indian philosophers mean by the world? Does it refer to any specific reality like water or earth? Generally speaking, the world in the Indian philosophical tradition stands for a concept or an idea, or refers to all that is there (*viśvam* or *sarvam*).[1] It is not simply a collection or totality of facts or phenomena, but in a sense their unity or oneness. All the facts or phenomena we know or experience constitute the world. And if at all we can think of a reality that can limit or determine the world it is space, and space is limitless. World and space are co-extensive. We cannot think of the world without space, and yet space is known by the world or by the things or phenomena that

---

1. The Sanskrit words *viśvam* or *sarvam* convey the sense of the world, and they mean all that is there. However, there are other words in Sanskrit which also mean world like *prapañca*, *jagat* and *loka*, but these do not convey the sense of the world as the words *viśvam* and *sarvam* convey. The words like *papañca* either try to determine the extension of the world, or some value is imposed on the world. *Jagat* stands for what is moving, and *loka* means a realm.

constitute the world. Therefore the world, according to Indian philosophy, means a unity or a whole in which all the things or phenomena find their place and unity. Such a philosophical conception of the world, as all that is there (*sarvam* or *viśvam*), is not really compatible with any theological or metaphysical view in which the reality of the world is sought to be explained in terms of another reality, or in which some reality other than and beyond the world is postulated as the explanation or the cause of the world. In the Indian tradition, a human being is taken as an analogy to understand the world, the unity or oneness of all that is there, as in a human being all the basic elements of the world find their representation and unity. And man is not regarded or seen as a mechanical unity of the elements of the world. He has an identity which cannot be reduced to or explained in terms of any one of the aspects or elements that constitute his person. His unity represents, in a very subtle form, the unity of all that is there, and as the unity of a person transcends the elements that constitute his being, the unity of the world is also more than the facts or phenomena that constitute the world. We find in the Indian philosophical tradition another term *prakṛti* (nature) to mean the world. However, like the terms *sarvam* or *viśvam*, *prakṛti* does not mean the world or all that is there. It is meant to explain the physical or non-spiritual realm or side of the world, whereas the idea of the world comprehends both the realms (*prakṛti* and *puruṣa*) or all that is there.

As stated earlier, we find in the Indian philosophical tradition, two basically different ways of understanding the world. As causal explanation plays a significant role in understanding the things or phenomena of the world most of the philosophers think that causal explanation is equally significant in understanding the world and its nature. Therefore, most of the philosophers, in order to understand the world, try to find a causal explanation for its existence, or seek to know or understand that which is the ultimate cause of the world. They are guided by the law of causation in understanding the world, and think that the world cannot exist by itself. The world must have been caused to exist as in the world of empirical experience things cannot exist by themselves; they are caused to exist. We find several forms of causation in the world of empirical experience such as transformation, evolution, manifestation, etc. and all these forms of causation are seen as significant in knowing or understanding the world, especially the physical realm or aspect of the world. However, we get a different meaning of causation when we try to understand artefacts, or all those things which depend for their existence on human agency. Human agency is involved in such things as arts, literature, music and the various forms of culture which are the varied forms of expression of human intelligence and creativity. In relation to or in the light of these we get a new or different meaning of causation though it may not be significant in understanding the physical realm or aspect of the world. In other words, causation which is meaningful at the physical level or in explaining the physical realm of the world may not be meaningful or significant in understanding the reality in which human creativity is involved. Therefore, even if we admit that causal explanation of the world is significant in understanding the world, any one form or mode of causation is not significant in explaining the existence of the world.

In the other way of understanding the world, the object is not so much to find a causal explanation for the existence of the world as to know or understand its true or real nature. While in the former way of understanding the world philosophers have taken for granted that the nature or reality of the world is what it is known through empirical experience and knowledge, in the other way of understanding the world, philosophers think that the true or real nature of the world is not fully and clearly known through empirical knowledge or experience. It is possible that the nature of the world as it is known empirically is not its true or real nature, or the true or real nature of the world is not fully and clearly revealed through sense-knowledge. Although we depend primarily upon empirical experience and knowledge to know or understand the world, yet it is possible that something very significant about the world or its nature is not known or accessible to our empirical knowledge and experience. Otherwise, there would have been no philosophical or scientific quest to know or understand the world. People then would have contented themselves with what they know about the world empirically. Now, it is one thing to think that a philosophical or metaphysical quest to know the real or true nature of the world cannot be satisfied or fulfilled, and another to think that the quest itself is meaningless or futile. Although the world is known to all it remains a mystery to some philosophers as there is no definite and universally acceptable knowledge or understanding of the world and its nature. And until we know what is the true or real nature of the world it is presumptuous on our part to think that the world cannot exist by itself, or has no independent existence. The fact that things in the world come into existence, or are governed by the law of causation is no reason to think that the world as such has also come into existence, or is governed by the law of causation. And in thinking so we create another reality or world to understand the world of our empirical experience. The fact that matter is the causal explanation of various material or physical objects is no justification to think that the existence of matter must also have a causal explanation. These we discuss more fully elsewhere.

Before we discuss the two ways of understanding the world we have to discuss, though briefly, the nature and meaning of causation, according to Indian philosophical tradition, as it plays a very significant role in one way of understanding the world. Broadly speaking, two major problems are involved in understanding causation. Firstly, how to recognize something as an effect or as caused, and how to understand the nature of the relationship between a cause and the effect? In the case of artefacts it is easy to recognize them as caused or as effects because they are not to be found in the natural world. They are not part of or do not constitute the natural world. Moreover, we can observe the production of artefacts, such as golden ornaments, clay-pots, etc. and the process can be repeated. We know how gold or clay is transformed into various objects. But we do not observe the formation of mountains, rivers, stones, etc. though we know that they are also formed or are brought into existence. Rivers, mountains, stones, etc. are not artefacts though they come into existence. We know or understand that they are caused to exist or brought into existence because of their composite nature. A stone or a mountain or a river is a composite reality because it can be analysed into its parts. A river is composed of several drops of water, and a mountain of several particles though we do not observe the formation of a mountain or a river. Nevertheless, we know that they are caused or come into existence due to joining or coming together of the parts or elements that make them. The point we are trying to make is that in the case of the things that constitute the world we can observe both cause and effect before we try to understand the causal relationship between them. For instance, in making golden objects all the gold is not involved, or all the clay is not transformed into clay-objects so that we cannot see gold or clay independently of the objects made of gold or clay. But if we see golden objects only, but not the gold, how to identify gold as their cause. However, we observe in the world causes and their effects, and in several cases we can also observe the causes giving rise to effects. In other words, in most cases we can determine the cause of a thing.

In the case of the world we see the world only but not its cause, and therefore our knowledge or understanding of the cause of the world is a matter of understanding. But do we have some ground or basis in the world of empirical experience that can help in identifying the cause of the world, as the reality that is supposed to be the cause of the world must not have remained unaffected in giving birth to the world so that we can know it independently of the world? And as the existence of the world precedes the existence of human beings there is no possibility of anyone observing the world coming into existence. But before we discuss the problem of the world coming into existence, we have to discuss whether the world can or cannot exist by itself. It would be meaningful to discuss the problem of causation with regard to the world only when we can prove or show that the world cannot exist by itself, or has no independent existence. How can we know whether the world has an independent existence or not? How can we say that the world cannot exist by itself, or is caused to exist? Even if we think that the world is caused to exist we have to understand the sense in which it is caused to exist. The world as we know it is dynamic or undergoes change in the sense the forms of things that constitute the world go on changing as some forms are destroyed and newer forms come into existence. Nevertheless, the world seems to exist unchanged in the sense the basic elements that constitute the world remain unaffected by the change in forms. Gold does not undergo change in its nature when it undergoes change in its forms. We can therefore identify gold in all its forms, or in all the objects of gold as its nature remains unchanged as change occurs only in its form. On the other hand, if change occurs in the nature of gold along with the change in its form we cannot identify gold in its different forms. As we can identify gold as the substance that is present commonly in all the objects of gold, we cannot identify the substance that is present in all the things of the world for the simple reason that the world is not homogeneous. The various things that constitute the world do not share the same substance. We cannot say that the same substance is present or is being manifested in all the things or phenomena of the world as gold is present in all the objects of gold. The differences in the things or objects of the world point to differences in substance as the different objects of the world cannot be explained in terms of difference in form. Now, in the case of the natural things of the world we can relate cause and effect on the basis of the substance they share or manifest. The cause and effect differ only in their forms, but not in their substance. On the other hand, if two things differ in their substance, even if they have the same form, we cannot relate them as cause and effect. In other words, the cause and effect are different only in form, but not in substance, as they share the same substance or the same substance is present in both of them. The clay is the substance of all the objects of clay as clay is present in all the objects of clay. Now, can we say that all the things or phenomena of the world share the same substance so that we can think of that substance as the cause of the world, or trace the origin of the world to that substance?

Whether all the substances like gold, clay, etc. which we find in the world, can be subsumed under one substance, or be regarded as the manifestations of a single substance, is a metaphysical problem to which we find several solutions. However, according to popular understanding all the things of the world can be reduced to or explained in terms of certain basic elements like earth, fire and water, as these basic elements are regarded as sufficient to explain the different things we find in the world. Whether these elements can find their explanation in a single substance or reality is not a problem for the popular mind. However, some philosophers think that these elements are basically atomic in structure, and therefore the world is constituted of atoms. But we are not going to discuss the various metaphysical theories propounded to explain the existence of the world as it is not our main concern. Our main concern is whether the world is caused to exist or can be explained in terms of a single substance or reality. And the basic problem with which most of the Indian philosophers are concerned is whether the existence of the world can be explained in terms of a single reality or substance, and if so what could be its nature. According to some of the Indian philosophers, the existence of the world can be explained in terms of a single substance or reality called matter which in terms of its dynamism can manifest or transform itself into the world of multiplicity. We discuss in a separate chapter the nature of matter, according to Indian philosophy, and the possibility of its being the substance or reality of the world.[2] However, according to some of the Indian philosophers, matter is sufficient to explain the world as it is the predominant reality of the world. Almost all the things and phenomena of the world are physical or material as matter constitutes their reality. Matter seems to be the substance of the world as it is present in almost all the things and phenomena of the world when compared to spirit or consciousness whose presence is limited to the realm of living beings, or more specifically to human beings. Consciousness is present in almost all the living beings as simple awareness, while in human beings it is more fully and clearly revealed. In human beings, consciousness is recognized as a reality by itself as it cannot be explained in terms of physical reality of man. We discuss the problem whether consciousness can be explained in terms of matter in another chapter.[3] However, with the exception of those, according to whom matter is the only reality, and that is sufficient to explain the world, including consciousness, most of the philosophers think that it is not possible to explain consciousness in terms of matter. Although some of the philosophers have not seen any problem in explaining human mind and its various functions in terms of human body or matter they find it difficult or rather impossible to explain consciousness in terms of human body or matter as they find opposition between matter and consciousness. In their natures matter and consciousness are opposed to each other, or the opposition between them is fundamental. While consciousness is essentially a subject or the principle of awareness matter is always an object to consciousness, and therefore one can never become the other, or one cannot be the explanation of the other. However, these problems are discussed in detail in the chapter on

---

2. See chapter on Matter.
3. See chapter on Consciousness.

consciousness. Those who are opposed to each other in terms of their nature cannot be the explanation of one another, as to be related causally the cause and effect must share the same substance or reality, or the same substance should form the reality of both which is not, however, the case with matter and consciousness.

Now, if matter cannot be the explanation of consciousness then it cannot be *Brahman*, the reason for the existence of the world, which includes consciousness. And the easy way out of the problem of opposition between matter and consciousness is to accept the independent existence of matter and consciousness. Thus the Sāṁkhya philosophy tried to understand and explain the existence of the world in terms of the duality of matter and spirit which are ultimately real. We need not discuss here all the arguments against Sāṁkhya metaphysics. But we can point out to some of the major problems involved in understanding the Sāṁkhya metaphysics. Sāṁkhya accepts the independent existence of matter and spirit as one cannot be the explanation of the other or one cannot be reduced to the other because they are opposed to each other in their natures. But how can they come together or unite themselves for the purpose of evolution of the world? By conceiving matter in dynamic terms Sāṁkhya could explain that the evolution of matter as internal dynamism of matter is sufficient to explain the evolution of matter, the reason for the existence of the world of multiplicity. But in that case the evolution of matter can have no beginning. It will be a beginningless process, and therefore having no end in view. We cannot then think of a beginning to the world process, and therefore there is no need to explain the existence of the world as it has not come into existence. However, the crucial problem, according to Sāṁkhya, is how to explain the reality of man in whom both matter and spirit are present and are united. When they can co-exist in man we have to admit that there can be no opposition between them. Two realities which are opposed to each other in their natures cannot come together or be united to initiate the process of evolution of the world of which man is an integral part. Moreover, as, according to Sāṁkhya, spirit has no purpose to accomplish, its coming together with matter serves no purpose either of its own or that of matter. Matter on its own can evolve as it is inherently dynamic. But how to understand the existence of spirit before the start of evolution? Spirit as an independent reality must have its own existence. One of the points of opposition between spirit and matter is that the former is not in space. It does not occupy space as it is not a physical reality. It is only matter that occupies space. If spirit does not exist in space as it is not a physical reality then we must admit that it somehow exists in matter, as in the reality of man. If the spirit does not occupy space, how can we relate it to matter as without being related to matter it cannot influence matter in the process of evolution? We do not find spirit that is disembodied. In the world of empirical experience, like energy, spirit is always found in association with a body. How then to understand the independent existence of spirit, or its existence before it got itself entangled in a human body? All the arguments of Sāṁkhya for the existence of spirit are relevant and meaningful only in relation to the existence of individual spirit or self which is embodied.[4] But the spirit before it is embodied or before it has acquired an individuality is free from matter or is disembodied, and that kind of state is also the cherished goal or destiny of spirit, according to Sāṁkhya. Can spirit exist by itself? And if by

4. In the Sāṁkhya philosophy the only justification for accepting the independent existence of spirit or *puruṣa* is that the matter cannot explain the existence of spirit because of the opposition between matter and spirit. The arguments we find in the *Sāṁkhya-Kārikā* are significant only in relation to the spirit that is embodied or mixed up with *prakṛti*. Before the evolution *puruṣa* has no relation with *prakṛti*. It is only after evolution *puruṣa* finds itself related to *prakṛti*, and therefore the arguments are significant only in relation to the *puruṣa* after evolution. The argument like the composite reality (*prakṛti*) is meant to serve the purpose of someone other than the composite reality (*puruṣa*); *puruṣa* is required to preside over and govern what is composite in nature; there must be an enjoyer of *prakṛti* in its state of evolution; and finally the process of evolution works for the purpose of release of *puruṣa*. (*Sāṁkhya-Kārikā*, verse 17).

spirit we do not mean the individual spirit that lives in man we cannot think of limits to its existence. Can we say that spirit is as pervasive or omnipresent as matter before the start of evolution? And if both matter and spirit are equally pervasive before the start of evolution, the influence of one upon the other or the relationship between matter and spirit must be conceived as something natural, but not as induced by either. In that case also the process of evolution must have no beginning, and hence no end. If the spirit and matter are always together as they occupy the same space the process of evolution can have no beginning or an end. On the other hand, if by spirit the Sāṁkhya means the individual or embodied spirit, as all the Sāṁkhya arguments are relevant in relation to it only, then we cannot think of spirit that is disembodied. Although we can think of disembodied spirit as we can of pure energy we do not come across spirit that is without a body. Thus the dualistic metaphysics of Sāṁkhya, which has left a deep influence on the development of Indian metaphysics, could not, however, provide a satisfactory explanation for the existence of the world.

The problem of the relationship between spirit and matter, which Sāṁkhya could not explain satisfactorily, was later felt by Ramanuja and Sri Aurobindo, who in their own ways tried to integrate matter and spirit in *Brahman*.[5] Since matter cannot be the explanation of spirit, and spirit the matter, and as both are required to explain the world, they tried to understand them as being integral to the nature of *Brahman*. According to them, both matter and spirit constitute the nature of *Brahman*. While matter

5. Sri Ramanuja and Sri Aurobindo tried to find place for both matter and consciousness in the reality of *Brahman*. According to Sri Ramanuja, while matter forms the body of *Brahman*, the spirit is the self of *Brahman*. Thus as the body and self of *Brahman*, matter and spirit form the person of *Brahman* who is the unity of both matter and spirit. According to Sri Aurobindo, *Brahman* has two fundamental aspects which correspond to matter and spirit, and that explains the world which consists of matter and consciousness. Sri Aurobindo also thinks that matter is sleeping spirit.

forms the body or the physical aspect of *Brahman*, the spirit is seen as the soul or self of *Brahman*. In other words, conceived as a personal being, on the analogy of a human person, *Brahman* is viewed as a unity or oneness of both matter and spirit. In the world of empirical experience it is in the human reality that both matter and spirit are integrated. Man is the unity of matter and spirit. By conceiving *Brahman* in personal terms or as a personal being so as to overcome the problem of relationship between spirit and matter the basic problem of opposition between matter and spirit is overlooked. The reality of man is a fact, and in him both matter and spirit are integrated. He is neither body nor spirit but an embodied spirit. Is then the problem of opposition between matter and spirit purely conceptual or metaphysical as in man we find their unity? If Sāṁkhya, which is really philosophical in its approach and understanding, finds it difficult to relate matter and spirit in any manner, can we really overcome the opposition between them by attributing them to *Brahman* or by conceiving them as forming the body and self of *Brahman*? For the sake of argument, it may be pointed out that the opposition between matter and sprit is real or meaningful only at the empirical level, as at that level only the spirit is a knower or a subject and matter is the object of experience or knowledge. But the opposition between matter and spirit may not be real at a higher or transcendental level. At a higher or transcendental level they may find their unity in the person of *Brahman* who is beyond or transcends the categories of empirical knowledge and understanding. Now, if matter and spirit can find their unity in *Brahman*, be it personal or impersonal, one or two significant things must follow. If *Brahman* is the ultimate explanation of the world or all that is there then the nature of *Brahman* must be present or reflected in all that is there. But we find the unity of matter and spirit only in the reality of man. Can we then say that man is the best form of manifestation of *Brahman*, or is he the culmination of the process of *Brahman*'s evolution? Can we say that the reality of *Brahman* is more fully and clearly revealed in the reality of man?

Accepting that man as the best form of manifestation of *Brahman* in the world of empirical experience how to understand and explain the absence of spirit, a basic or essential aspect of *Brahman*'s reality, in much of the world? Much of the world as we know it is devoid of spirit or consciousness even in its most rudimentary form. And if *Brahman* is to be the causal explanation of the world process we cannot understand why much of the world is devoid of *Brahman*'s nature. Can we think of *Brahman*'s nature being partially present in some realms of the world, and fully in some other realms? If it is possible to think that the nature of *Brahman* is equally present within the physical as well as the spiritual realms of the world, for which there is no empirical evidence, we have to admit a split or division in the nature or reality of *Brahman*. Then it vitiates the oneness or unity of *Brahman*. On the other hand, if *Brahman*, like the God of theologians, is conceived as the creator of the world. He need not be present in the world. He can create the world by merely wishing it to be. It is meaningful theologically to think of *Brahman* as the creator of the world as in that case his will is sufficient to explain the existence of the world. He need not then be present in the world. However, such theological assertions depend for their justification or validity entirely on faith in scriptures. But philosophically speaking if the world and *Brahman* do not share the same reality or substance, or if the reality of the world is not the same as that of *Brahman*, it is not possible to rationally justify *Brahman* as the cause of the world, as to be causally related the cause and effect must have or share the same substance.

However, we find some philosophical justification for the positions of Ramanuja and Sri Aurobindo. It is only in the realm of living beings, or more specifically in human reality, we find the presence of spirit or consciousness. Man is both physical and spiritual, or in him both matter and spirit are united. As we can find pure matter in the world we cannot find pure spirit or disembodied consciousness in the world. What justification can we then have to think that spirit or consciousness has an independent existence? If consciousness has an independent existence it must be able to manifest itself independently of matter or human body which, however, is not the case. And if pure spirit is a myth then the spirit or consciousness must be viewed as being integral to human body which is not simply matter. We find consciousness in all living beings though it is not as clearly and perfectly revealed in them as in a human being. A body, be it that of an animal or man, is more than matter as spirit is integral to it. A human being is neither pure matter nor pure spirit; he is a unity of both. Though we can distinguish physical aspect of man from consciousness we cannot separate them. And consciousness is not a part of man like any of his limbs because consciousness in man cannot be localized, and it has no specific function as that of any part of the body. It is present in all that a man does and thinks. We may be able to conceive consciousness as having a reality of its own as we can think of any universal, but they are not known independently of a thing or a phenomenon. More importantly, man as a personal being is distinct from all other living beings, and if his existence is to find an explanation in the reality of *Brahman*, then *Brahman* must be a personal being. And personality or the personal character of man involves both body and spirit. While spirit or consciousness is what is universal in man, his body, including mind, gives him a personal identity or individuality. Therefore, the reality of man cannot be explained either in terms of matter or in terms of spirit as in his person both are integrated. Therefore to be a satisfactory or sufficient explanation of the world or all that is there *Brahman* must also be the explanation of human reality. And if we regard man as the epitome of the world process it is all the more necessary why we should conceive *Brahman* as the unity or integration of both matter and spirit. This can be sufficient justification for conceiving *Brahman* as a personal being in whom both matter and spirit are united and integrated. And if both matter and spirit are inseparable in the nature of *Brahman* that should be the case with the world also as *Brahman* being the essence or self of the world it should be immanently present in the world.

Now, can we think of evolution purely in terms of matter? We know that matter undergoes change in the sense that it gets itself transformed into various things in terms of its own dynamic character. For instance, mountains, rocks, oceans and other material objects are the forms of matter, and the inner dynamism of matter is sufficient to explain their existence. No other cause is required to explain their existence. The whole of physical reality with all its diversity can find its explanation in matter, or matter is sufficient to explain the existence of the world, with the exception of spirit or consciousness. However, highly significant attempts have been made to explain spirit or consciousness in terms of matter, and if matter is sufficient to explain consciousness there will be no need to think of another reality other than matter to explain the existence of the world. We discuss this problem comprehensively when we try to understand the nature of matter as conceived by several Indian philosophers and the possibility of its being the ultimate explanation of the world.[6] Is it meaningful to think of evolution purely in terms of matter? Matter undergoes change, and we find different forms of change. And no one form of change is sufficient to understand and explain the existence of the world. We find several forms of change taking place in matter. A small pebble or stone is not different from a hill or mountain in substance as they differ only in their forms. Simple change is not purposeful as it is devoid of any design. But evolution involves some design or purpose in the sense that things grow or evolve themselves to realize what is inherently there within themselves. A seed grows itself into a tree in the sense that what is potentially present in the seed is actualized, and the process of realization or actualization is known as evolution. The purpose involved in the process of evolution is not extrinsic to it. And any kind of change

6. See chapter on Matter.

in matter, including evolution, is due to the nature of matter, but not imposed on matter from outside. Now, evolution also is a change of form of matter and is meaningful in terms of actualization of what is potentially there in matter. In growing into a tree what is potential in a seed is actualized, or we can say metaphorically the seed realizes itself in becoming a tree. While at the physical level evolution means simple change in the forms of matter, at the organic level it means growth which reaches its culmination in man. There is growth in man also which is meaningful at the physical level, however, at the level of mind or consciousness growth or development means self-realization of man. Human evolution is more meaningful at the mental or spiritual level as the growth at the physical level is almost predetermined. Human evolution at the mental or spiritual level leads to self-realization on the part of man which some philosophers consider as the culmination of the evolution itself. Evolution or growth leading to self-realization is a conscious process and is therefore a free process. Now, we cannot say whether at any stage in the process of evolution any reality other than matter has intervened so that evolution has taken a different or conscious turn. Whether evolution is a conscious process or not is a different problem. When a seed grows itself into a tree it is not conscious of its growth as man is conscious of his mental growth. An animal also grows without being aware of its growth. This is also the case with man as far as his physical growth is concerned. Only in the realm of mind or more specifically of spirit we can think of growth which is conscious and hence free. In other words, to be purposeful growth must be conscious and free which is possible in the case of man only. How far is it then meaningful to say that the world as we know or experience it, which includes the evolution of man, is simply due to evolution of matter? Is it not meaningful to think that the evolution of man or his spirit is integral to the evolution of matter? It is only with the emergence of man the problem of spirit arises, and if the emergence of man is part of the evolution of matter we have to think of matter and its nature in fundamentally different terms. However, from the point of view of empirical experience it may appear meaningless to think that the evolution of matter takes a conscious turn at a stage in the process of evolution. This problem can be decided only when we know for certain the true nature of matter.

However, what is possible in the case of matter is its inner dynamism. It undergoes change in the sense that the forms of its existence are changed. Several things come into existence due to change in the forms of matter, or the world of multiplicity is due to change in the forms of matter. Evolution is also a change of form of matter. Artefacts also point to change in the forms of matter, but the artefacts are humanly designed. In the case of artefacts human agency is involved, and much of the world consists of such artefacts. Change is natural to matter or matter is inherently dynamic. It is a different problem whether the dynamism of matter is sufficient to explain the process of evolution which is conscious. However, the world in which humans live is a limited part of the world in which evolution is self-conscious. But the emergence of man is a very significant event in the process of evolution, and therefore whether man is a product of evolution of matter is also a crucial problem which we discuss separately.

We now discuss the ontological status of matter. Is matter a created reality or is it an independent reality? Can matter exist by itself or is it caused to exist? How to approach and understand this problem? How can we know whether matter is caused to exist or not? There is no direct evidence to show that matter is caused. However, we can know whether a thing is caused or not by understanding the nature of the thing. If a thing is a composite reality we can infer that it is brought into existence by combining its parts. And we can know that a thing is composite when we can analyse it into its parts or components till we reach the simplest elements which cannot be analysed any further. A pebble or stone has no independent existence because it can be analysed into small particles. A pool of water is a combination of several drops of water. Now these particles or drops can be further analysed, and in the process we arrive at atoms or simple elements. An atom is defined as the simplest thing or reality which cannot be analysed further, and matter is constituted of such atoms. And atoms are not caused to exist as they can exist by themselves. They are uncaused since we cannot prove otherwise. In a way they are the ultimate explanation of the world as matter is atomic in structure. Thus matter is caused in one sense, and is not caused in another sense. Matter is caused in the sense that it is due to the combination of atoms, and is not caused because the atoms which are the reality of matter are not caused. Atoms and matter are not really different. Although atoms constitute matter we do not perceive them as we see matter in its different forms. However, matter as such is not an object of experience, though it is the cause of the world in the sense that much of the world is matter in its different forms.

There is another strong reason to think that matter is not caused to exist. We do not really see matter as such, but we see different things which we regard as different forms of matter. Matter is the reason for the existence of different forms which constitute the world, and when we talk of matter we usually talk of the forms of matter as mater as such is not an object of perception. Matter undergoes change in acquiring different forms as without change in matter the different forms of matter cannot come into existence. As the world of empirical experience is constituted of the different forms of matter the world comes into existence along with the change in matter which is due to its own dynamism. Can we therefore say that the matter as we know or understand it, that is the different forms of matter, is caused by matter which we do not directly see? And as the forms of matter constitute the world we can say that the world is in a sense caused by matter as it cannot exist without the various things that are the forms of matter. Can there be any reason for the matter to change itself into various forms? Since matter is devoid of consciousness in any form we cannot say that the change is purposive. We cannot think of matter willing to change itself into different forms. On the other hand, if we think that change in matter is a natural process we cannot think of a beginning to the process of change in matter. Change must then be viewed as having no beginning. And if change in matter has no beginning then we cannot say that matter is the cause of its forms, or the forms are caused by matter. Therefore, the world as the totality of forms of matter cannot be regarded as caused by matter. Matter and world are co-eternal, and therefore we cannot say that the world has come into existence, or the matter has caused the world to exist. On the other hand, when matter exists in itself or without any change then we cannot call it world. It is only when matter changes itself into various forms that the world of empirical experience comes into existence. Any change in matter is sufficient to call it world. And if we want to think of matter without forms we have to explain why it starts changing itself. The Sāṁkhya tried to explain the beginning of the process of change of matter in terms of the spirit which in a sense acts as the prime mover. But in the absence of spirit we have to admit that the process of change in matter has no beginning, and therefore there is no sense in saying that the world is caused to exist by matter or matter is the cause of the world. It would be meaningful to think of the world coming into existence when matter can exist without change, as the change in matter is the reason for the existence of the world. If we are willing to accept this position we have to posit another reality which is supposed to be the cause of the change in matter and the reason for it to cause change in matter. Such thinking instead of solving any problem ends in creating more problems.

2

Approach to World II

In the previous chapter we tried to understand a more dominant and also a more popular way of understanding the world in which the law of causation plays a significant role. Our understanding of the world is guided or influenced by the laws or principles which regulate and govern the world of our empirical experience of which the law of causation is an important one. In this chapter we discuss the other significant way of understanding the world in which the major concern is not so much to find a causal explanation for the existence of the world as to know or understand the real or true nature of the world. Most of the Indian philosophers think that the reality of the world is what it is revealed to us in our empirical experience, and the only problem with regard to the world, according to them, is its origin. Therefore most of the philosophers try to understand the origin of the world, or to find a causal explanation for its existence. However, according to some of the prominent philosophers, the nature of the world as it is known empirically may not be its real or true nature. Although our understanding of the world is based mainly on our experience of it, the role of reason in understanding the world is equally significant as it helps in organizing and integrating our experience of the world. We get the sense of the world only when the various things and phenomena we experience are organized and integrated, as the world as such is not an object of experience. World stands for the unity or oneness of all that we experience and is therefore a concept or an idea. To know or understand the world, therefore, does not mean to know or understand the things or phenomena we experience. We soon discuss what makes us think that the different things and phenomena we experience belong to or constitute the world. And if the world is only a concept or an idea, trying to know or understand its true or real nature does not have sense or meaning. At the same time, to know or understand the true nature of the world does not mean knowing the true or real nature of any particular thing or phenomenon we experience. On the other hand, if we think that the world refers to a reality which is not the same as the reality of different things or phenomena we experience, we must be able to justify its existence. But if we think that there is no reality which unites or integrates all the things or phenomena we experience into one whole, there will be no meaning in trying to know or understand the real or true nature of the world.

What is the sense in which the world is a concept or an idea? It is not similar to a concept, like man or tree, as it does not represent anything experienced in the world. The world, as it stands for all that is there, cannot be an object of experience. It also does not stand in relation to any other reality, as it cannot be differentiated or distinguished from anything else as by definition the world is all that is there. For instance, *prakṛti* and *puruṣa* of Sāṁkhya are two independent concepts, and are meaningful by themselves. Although abstract in nature they are based on what is experienced. *Prakṛti* stands for the nature or the physical side or aspect of the world, and *puruṣa* stands for the spiritual aspect or side of the world. And both are independent realities. One cannot comprehend or include the other, but both are comprehended or included in the concept of world. The world means both of them as the world comprehends both of them. However, the world apparently means a spatial unity or unity in space of several things and phenomena which we experience. The space and time which comprehend and affect all that we experience and know may help in understanding the unity of all that is there or the world. But when we talk of unity or oneness of the world we are not referring to such unity. What we mean by the unity or oneness of the world is the unity of substance of all that is there. Is there any substance or reality which by being present in all that is there binds them together and forms the unity or oneness of all that is there? Can we think of a substance or reality which is the reality of all that is there, and is therefore present inherently in all that we know and experience? Is there anything, to express in the language of the Upaniṣads, by knowing which all that is there is known?[1] Although the unity of all that is there is not evident to us in terms of our empirical experience its possibility cannot be denied. If the world is not simply a collection or combination of discrete facts but something more, we have to investigate and understand in what sense the world is more than the things and phenomena we experience empirically. And if we think of the world as the unity of all that is there in terms of a reality that unites all by being the reality of all, a philosophical enquiry into the existence and nature of that reality is both legitimate and meaningful. And in knowing it we not only come to know the true nature of the world, but its unity as well, or the sense in which the world or all that is there is one. However, the substance or reality of all that is empirically real is not directly revealed to our empirical experience. The reality of what is empirically real is what we mean by the true or real nature of what is empirically real or the world, and as the true nature of what is empirically real is not something other than what is empirically real the problem of proving its existence does not arise.

Now, if there is a substance or reality common to all that is empirically real or the world then its nature must be reflected in all that we know and experience. And if one and the same substance or reality is the reality of all that is there, there can be no conflict or opposition among things we experience. But as pointed out in the previous chapter we find opposition between matter and spirit which is irreconcilable. And because of the

1. *Muṇḍaka Upaniṣad*, 1.1.3.

opposition between them one cannot be the explanation of the other, and more importantly, both cannot find their explanation in one and the same reality, or one and the same reality cannot be the reality of both matter and spirit. Then what makes us think that the nature of the world as empirically experienced may not be its true or real nature. If the nature of the world as revealed to us in our empirical experience is the true nature of the world, or our empirical experience reveals the true or real nature of the world there is no sense in trying to know the real or true nature of the world. Are we in any sense trying to deny or doubt the reality of the world when we try to know the true or real nature of the world of our empirical experience? What is it to know the true or real nature of what we experience ? What makes us think that the nature of the world as we know or experience it empirically may not be its true or real nature? Can we say that the problem arises mainly because of the confusion in the use of the word "real"? How to understand the meaning of "real"? Can we know or understand the meaning of "real" or "true" independently of our experience? If, in understanding or defining the meaning of these terms, our experience of the world is not really relevant or significant, what makes us, in the first place, to doubt the reality or truth of what we experience? Can we understand and define the terms independently of our experience of the world? If that is possible they can then mean anything, or they do not have a meaning which is commonly acceptable. And in that case trying to know the real or true nature of what is known as real will be superficial. Before we discuss this problem let us try to understand the reason why we doubt the reality of what we know or experience empirically. If it is not a mere assumption that the world we experience is not really real, or is not a sort of value which we want to impose on the world we experience, we have to find out the reasons why some philosophers doubt the reality of the world of empirical experience. What is real, or how to understand the meaning of "real"? In the Indian philosophical tradition "real" (*sat*) and "true" (*satyam*) are used mostly as synonyms. They are cognate words. What is real is true though the meaning of true is wider than real. How to define what is real? Normally, we accept as real anything that exists, or real is that which exists. And when we make the assertion that what exists is real our assertion is true, but not when we assert as true what does not exist. Anything that exists is real. But how to know what exists? Can we assert that a thing which does not exist is real? In other words, what does not exist is not real. It may therefore appear self-evident that what exists is real, but it is not really so, because what exists is also a problem. How can we assert that a thing exists because the meaning of existence is not self-evident? Can we say that anything that is experienced exists because we cannot experience a thing which does not exist? But it may be pointed out that things which we experience need not be real as they may not exist. We experience things which are not real, but can we say that we experience a thing which does not exist? It is meaningful to say that we experience things which are not real, but it is not meaningful to say that we experience things which do not exist. In such cases it may appear that we make a subtle distinction between what exists and what is real. In the state of dream we experience things which we consider as having no reality, as the reality of things we experience in dream depends upon dream state; they cease to be real the moment the dream is over. But can we say that the objects of dream experience do not exist? Can we experience an object that does not exist? If we can experience an object that does not exist we will not be able to say anything about it, or describe it. Such an experience cannot be regarded as an experience as it does not have a content which we can describe or communicate. But the fact that one can communicate one's dream experience as clearly as one can communicate his waking experience shows that the dream experience is related to or about the objects that exist. We can rather say that the objects of dream experience exist *per se*, and are therefore real *per se* though in relation to one's notion or understanding of what is real they may not be real. In other words, we try to understand and judge the validity of what is experienced in terms of an idea or a concept. And to bring in some extrinsic factor in judging the reality of a thing experienced leads us nowhere as it ends in infinite regress. Therefore, whatever we experience is real as we cannot experience a non-existent object. But how do we form the idea of real? Is it based on experience, or has nothing to do with experience? If it is based on experience it has to agree with experience or be consistent with experience. We cannot say that whatever is experienced during dream state is not real, or does not exist. If we do that we are trying to judge an experience on the basis of a notion or idea of what is real, which is unjustified, as no concept is formed independently of an experience. Therefore, the terms "real" and "exist" may mean the same as what exists is real or what is real must exist. But in the formation of the idea of real we bring in certain extraneous factors. We accept something as real when it does not depend for its existence on its being experienced. For instance, an illusory object depends for its existence on being experienced by someone who is under illusion, or a dream object on the one who dreams. According to this sort of understanding, the world of our empirical experience when viewed in relation to a mystical experience may prove to be unsubstantial.[2] The mystics' understanding of the world is different from that of our understanding, or the nature of the world as the mystics experience it is substantially different from that of our empirical experience. It is possible that someone who is intensely devoted to God, and

2. There is general agreement among the mystics belonging to different religious traditions of the world that the world of empirical experience is ephemeral and unsubstantial. The world cannot be the destiny of man as the spirit of man does not belong to the world. Man cannot find the meaning and fulfilment of his existence in the world of empirical experience. Ultimate fulfilment of man is not possible in this world as this is not the real world. Thus the world of empirical experience in the light of or in comparison with the mystical experience is ephemeral and unsubstantial. The world is not ultimately real.

has seen or realized Him may feel that the world of empirical experience is not real in the sense in which we understand the sense of real. Though both accept the reality of the world their understanding of its reality is not the same. However, both are experiences of the same reality. It is a different problem whether a mystical experience of the world is really objective as it may involve interpretation.

We also bring in the time factor in judging the validity of an experience. The dream experience is viewed as unreal only in relation to waking experience, or when compared to waking experience dream experience is short-lived. Similarly, those who do not doubt the validity of empirical experience start doubting it the moment they become mystics. The main reason why religious people and mystics look down upon the world of empirical experience is its temporal character when compared to mystical experience. In their language world is ephemeral. It is a different problem whether a religious or mystical experience is an objective experience, or an interpretation of an experience in which certain values are imposed on what we experience. However, certain insights are momentary or are flashes when compared to ordinary experiences, but prove themselves to be of great value. Similarly, the scientific understanding of the world differs significantly or even fundamentally from that of ordinary understanding though both are based on experience, and are about the same object. Thus we find two or more experiences of the same object which do not agree with each other, but they are real as they are experiences. How to judge the validity of an experience? The problem of validity of an experience does not arise when the objects of experience differ or are not the same, but when we come across different experiences of the same object the problem of judging their validity arises. We discuss this problem more fully in a different chapter. However, the problem we raised in the beginning about the validity of the empirical experience of the world is valid, for there are valid reasons to doubt the validity of the empirical experience of the world. When we are convinced that our understanding of the world, based on empirical experience, is not objective or is not true to its nature we are justified in trying to understand the real or true nature of the world.

It is only in relation to objects of waking experience that the objects of dream experience are not considered real because they last only as long as the dream lasts. In other words, when things can exist independently of their being experienced we regard them as truly or really existing. This is the attitude of mystics also towards the world of empirical experience or the mundane world. In other words, though the world of ordinary experience is real *per se* it ceases to be real in the light of or in relation to an experience in which the divine or God is realized. Even if we are prepared to grant validity to a mystical experience it does not help us in understanding the problem of reality, or what exists objectively. Every religion has a mystical tradition, and no two mystical traditions agree with each other on the nature of the object of mystical experience, or in what sense a mystical experience is an experience. Even within a religious tradition we find differences in the nature of reality which is mystically experienced. The fact that the mystics do not agree among themselves about the nature of reality that is experienced mystically means that we have no reason to believe in the objective nature of the reality that is mystically experienced. This can be true of the various views about the nature of ultimate reality expressed by different religious traditions which are inspired or are based either on a mystical experience or on a revelation. These views are not really intelligible to us unless we belong to and accept on faith the validity of such views.

However, there is a rational justification for doubting the reality of the world of empirical experience. Every object of empirical experience has two aspects, one that is changing, and the other that does not change. The objects undergo change, and at the same time we find something in the object that endures change, and because of which we are able to identify a thing, and name it. For instance, gold undergoes change in the sense that it undergoes change in its form. Though it acquires different forms we can identify gold in all its forms. And both these aspects of gold are real. The various forms in which we see gold are real, and at the same time gold which is present in all its forms is also real. Along with the change in its forms gold does not change its nature. We are not going to enter into discussion whether gold can exist without a form as that is not immediately relevant to our problem. We can identify gold in whatever form we may see it. Although we admit that both gold and its forms are real we make a distinction between gold and its forms, and the senses in which they are real. Gold retains its identity or nature in all the forms it acquires, and therefore, in whatever form we see gold we identify it. Gold may be seen in one form for a longer time, but that does not mean that form is intrinsic to gold. What remains the same or identical in all the forms of change is gold. More importantly, the forms depend upon gold for their reality as they cannot exist without gold, but that is not the case with gold. And even if we admit that gold cannot exist without a form, we cannot say that any one form is intrinsic to gold. In other words, gold does not depend for its existence on its forms as the forms depend upon gold for their existence or reality. We find different types of relationship between a substance and the forms it acquires. While the forms which the various things or phenomena acquire in the course of natural evolution are not imposed on them by a conscious agent, the forms which a purposive being, like man, imposes on them are purposeful. While the different forms rocks acquire in the course of natural evolution are not purposeful as they are not designed, the forms or shapes a sculptor carves in rocks are purposeful, for they are designed. Therefore the relationship between rocks formed during the course of geological evolution and their substance is different from the one in which a form is given to a rock by a sculptor. Natural facts are different from artefacts. But the relationship between forms and substance is the same whether the change is natural or produced. However, we are here concerned with the nature of relationship between the substance and the various forms it acquires, or the status of the substance in relation to the various forms it acquires. As pointed out earlier the forms can only have a dependent existence. They cannot exist by themselves as they are the forms of a substance, or forms cannot come into existence without a substance. It is a different problem whether pure forms or forms without a substance can exist. As most of the forms are universal, like the circle, we may say that the individual forms are copies of a form which can exist by itself. But that problem is not really relevant to our problem. However, unless a pure form is instantiated in experience, which involves substance, a pure form will have no existence. Here we have to make a distinction between the qualities or properties of a substance, and its changing forms. Both the qualities and the forms cannot exist without a substance as substance is the basis or substratum of both qualities and forms. While the qualities can belong to all the substances, no substance can be found with all the qualities. So is the case with the forms. Different substances, like gold or clay, can have the same form, and possess the same quality, but no quality or form can belong to any one substance exclusively.

What can be said about qualities and forms cannot be said about substances. However, what is common to various substances, like gold and clay, is the nature of the relationship they have with qualities and forms. As we are going to discuss, the relationship between a substance and its qualities or forms can only be logical as we cannot think of a substance and its qualities independently of each other; they cannot exist one without the other. In other words, they are not two independent realities that are related. We can think of a real relationship between them only when we can think of them independently of each other, or one without the other. But we cannot find a substance without a quality and form, and a quality or form without a substance. It is a different problem whether we can think of substance without qualities or forms and the qualities or forms without substance. When one cannot exist without the other to think of them as being related is not meaningful. It is only when one can exist without the other, or when two things are independently real, we can think of a relationship between them. On the other hand, when we cannot think of a substance without qualities and forms, and qualities or forms without a substance we have no reason to believe in their difference, and unless they are different they cannot be related. This problem gains more clarity when we think of self and its relation to human body. The problem of self is similar to the problem of substance as in both the cases we believe in something more than or beyond what we experience, for otherwise we think we cannot explain the individual existence of things or human beings. We discuss in a separate chapter whether man is more than his body and mind, and whether his self is different from his body and mind.[3] What justification do we have to believe in the existence of a self which is not the same as body-mind complex? Now, we can say something about the qualities and forms or describe them, but we cannot say anything about the substance except that it is the basis or substratum of the qualities. It has no real existence as it cannot be experienced and described. Can we think of existence independently of something that exists which can be experienced and described? Can we, in other words, separate a thing from its existence as if a thing comes into existence before it gets an identity in terms of its qualities or attributes? On the other hand, if we say that a thing must exist before it acquires its individuality in terms of certain qualities we are trying to separate the thing from its qualities as if the thing can exist without qualities and qualities without a thing.

However, we describe a substance in terms of the qualities and forms which we experience. In other words, we can talk of a

3. See chapter on Spirit.

substance only in terms of its qualities and forms as we do not know what substance is without the qualities and forms which we experience. As we cannot think of qualities existing by themselves we cannot also think of a substance devoid of qualities. It is not possible to think of the reality of a substance independently of its qualities and forms. Therefore, we cannot say that a substance has a reality of its own which is other than the reality of its qualities or attributes, or that a substance has a reality which is independent of its qualities and forms. The existence of a substance is therefore logical, as we find the problem only in thinking about things and their qualities. Substances and qualities do not hang in air before they come together, or are related. We think of a substance as that in which the qualities subsist or to which the qualities belong. For instance, gold is regarded as a substance to which certain qualities belong though we cannot think of gold without its qualities, as gold has no existence independently of its qualities. Therefore, when a substance undergoes change in its form the change affects the whole substance. When clay is transformed into pot the pot inherits all the characteristics of clay. Moreover, the clay ceases to exist when it has become a pot. Therefore, the only difference we find between clay and pot is only nominal. Clay is pot but with a change in form. However, there is a difference between a substance and its forms. A substance cannot be identified with its forms because substance is much more than its forms. No substance can be identified with any particular form. When clay becomes a pot the entire clay is not affected, only an amount of clay is transformed into pot, and is known as pot. There is no real difference between a substance, and the forms it acquires. A substance can acquire newer forms, and even when a specific form is destroyed the substance remains. If, on the other hand, the substance is to be identified with its forms then it should cease to exist when the forms are destroyed. Therefore, a substance is more than the forms it acquires, and though the substance is present in all the forms it cannot be identified with any of them. The transcendence of substance to its forms is only logical as no substance can ever be found without a form, and at the same time no form is intrinsic to a substance. The substance is much more than the forms in the sense it cannot be identified with any one form, and as a substance can acquire different forms no form can determine the substance.

However, that is not the case with the qualities. We cannot say that there are no qualities which are intrinsic to a substance as we can say that no form is intrinsic to a substance. We cannot find a substance without certain qualities, or certain qualities are natural to a substance as they are co-eternal with a substance; the substance is known in terms of those qualities. For instance, we cannot think of fire without heat or light or the capacity to burn though we can distinguish fire from heat, and light. Is it meaningful to say that fire is the substance and heat and light are its qualities. Fire and heat are inseparable, or one cannot exist without the other, and therefore we cannot relate them. This can be avoided if we can think of heat, light, and burning as forming the nature of fire instead of calling them the qualities of fire. Therefore, a substance is identified and even determined in terms of its qualities, or the substance is defined in terms of its qualities which are not different from it. Moreover, a substance is distinguished or differentiated from other substances in terms of qualities. Therefore, a substance does not transcend its qualities as a substance cannot be without its inherent qualities. A substance is not more than its inherent qualities as it cannot change or acquire its natural or inherent qualities. This also shows that the substance and its qualities are not different. A substance can however, acquire certain qualities which are not intrinsic to it. But a substance has no freedom with regard to its natural of inherent qualities.

We do not know what substance is independently of its qualities. The very definition of substance as that which is the basis (*āśraya*) or substratum of qualities or attributes shows that the qualities cannot exist without a substance. We do not experience qualities independently of a substance as the qualities cannot exist without a substance. As shown above the substance also cannot be known independently of its qualities. We can say something about the substance only in terms of its qualities as we cannot say anything about a substance which is devoid of qualities. However, a substance can also be the basis of certain qualities which it may acquire or lose, and we cannot therefore identify a substance in terms of such qualities. On the other hand, if a substance has only one quality it will not be possible to make a distinction between the substance and the quality. It is only when a substance has more than one quality it cannot be identified with any one quality. Now, a substance cannot have the same kind of relationship with its inherent qualities as it has with its forms. However, a substance can acquire certain qualities in addition to its inherent qualities. When a substance undergoes change in its form it acquires new attributes which are due to the change in its form. A pot has certain qualities which clay does not possess though pot is nothing but clay with a form. The attributes of a pot are not the attributes of clay, but it is clay which acquires the attributes because of the change in its form, and therefore in a sense the attributes of pot are the attributes which clay acquires. Therefore, a substance may acquire certain qualities because of the change in its form which it does not possess as substance. The acquired qualities can be attributed to the substance because it is the same substance that exists in all its forms. We can say acquired qualities are really related to the substance, as they change along with the change in the form of a substance. Whether the qualities are intrinsic or extrinsic to the substance they stand related to the substance in the same way; they depend for their existence on the substance. Substance is the basis for both kinds of qualities as without it they cannot exist. The qualities of a pot belong to clay, though not as clay. Though clay as clay cannot hold or contain things, as pot, a form of clay, it can hold or contain things. Such qualities can be indefinite as a substance can undergo various types of change.

What is then the nature of relationship between a substance and its qualities? Obviously the relationship is one of dependence, as the qualities, both natural and accidental, depend on the substance for their existence. But the dependence is only logical as the substance is not the reason or explanation for the existence of the qualities. And as we are maintaining all the while the qualities cannot exist without the substance as the qualities form the nature of the substance. Then there can be no relationship between them as they are not different. However, the qualities like colour, size, shape or form, etc. of a substance can change. But if all the qualities of a substance are accidental, and can be changed or destroyed we cannot then identify and name a substance. It is in terms of its inherent qualities a substance gets its identity and name. Gold is known by its inherent qualities as without them gold cannot be known and identified. Can we then say that a substance is a combination or composition of qualities or attributes? Is it the case that different substances emerge when qualities combine or associate themselves in various ways? But qualities do not exist by themselves. We do not observe qualities existing by themselves or independently of substances. It is only in the case of objects like a chariot we can say that they come into existence when the component parts are combined, and ceases to exist when the parts are separated. But that is not the case with a substance and its inherent qualities as we cannot think of a substance without its inherent qualities, and the qualities without the substance. They do not have independent existence.

If things can exist by themselves or independently of each other there can be a relationship between them which may be temporal or spatial. But when things cannot exist one without the other what ground do we have to think of a relationship between them? Can we say meaningfully that two things, which cannot be separated or which cannot exist independently of each other, are related? Is it meaningful to think of a relationship between things which cannot exist separately or independently of each other?

Can we think of a relation which has no beginning, and therefore no end? If at all such a relationship is possible it cannot be between two things or two realities. To be related things must have independent existence. Things which can exist independently can have a relationship, and that can be dissolved also. On the other hand, to think that things are eternally related or their relationship has no beginning, may mean that they are not really related. The fact that we can make a distinction between things is not sufficient justification to think that the things distinguished can exist by themselves or have an independent reality. Since we cannot think of qualities existing by themselves or independently of a substance we think that they can exist only by belonging to a substance or by forming the attributes of a substance, and if that is the valid reason for us to think of substance we can equally say that we cannot think of substance without or independently of qualities. And if we cannot think of substance and quality one without the other, or independently of each other there is no justification for us to think that they are different, or are related. If at all we can think of a relation between them that can only be a logical relationship. For instance, we can make a distinction between fire and heat, but that does not mean that they are two things which are related. However, in a sense, it is meaningful to think that they are different, as heat can be found in things other than fire. We cannot say that heat is related to fire only. When a thing is found in relation to more than one thing it is reasonable to think that its relationship with any one thing is not natural, or the two things are not really different. Heat is related to more than one thing. It is related to fire and the sun. And if we think that fire and the sun are two different substances or realities we are justified in thinking that they both possess a quality which is universal. In that case we cannot define a thing in terms of a quality whether it is intrinsic or accidental. However, the problem arises when we abstract a quality or attribute from a thing, and give it a sort of reality which it does not have.

Now, will there be any problem in trying to identify a thing of which heat is a quality as fire though existing or manifesting itself in different forms. We say sugar is sweet but there are so many things which are sweet, though in different degrees. Now, instead of seeing all the things which have the quality of sweetness as one substance we create several substances having the same quality of sweetness. Thus as we create the problem of relating an individual substance with a quality that is universal, we think that there are several substances which have the same quality. There is no problem in identifying the qualities which belong to several things, but how far are we justified in thinking of several substances having the same quality inherently? When a quality and the substance are inseparable what justification we can have in distinguishing substances having the same quality? When the same quality inheres in several things or when several things are known by the same quality there is no reason to think that they are different substances. The difference among such substances can only be numerical. On the other hand, if we can find some quality which is unique to a substance then we can think of several individual substances having qualities which are unique to each, but that is not the case in experience. But when there is nothing unique or particular about a substance there is no ground to distinguish it from other substances having the same qualities. Thus it is meaningful to say that a substance can acquire certain qualities while some qualities are natural to it. While the acquired qualities can be related to a substance, the intrinsic qualities are not related to the substance as they form its nature, and a thing cannot be without its nature. When a thing gives up its nature it ceases to be. A thing and its nature are not two things as they cannot be separated, or one cannot exist without the other. Thus a substance is known to exist in terms of its qualities, and the qualities help in defining the substance. On the other hand, if we think that substance is real or has its own existence independently of the qualities we must be able to identify it, and be able to say something about its nature. Can we think of a substance and identify it before it comes to possesses certain qualities and forms? In other words, can we think of a substance independently of its qualities? If we can think of substance as different from its qualities we must be able to understand its nature, and identify it. And if we think that substance has no nature of its own, and cannot therefore be defined independently of the qualities then to think of its independent existence, and then trying to understand its existence in relation to qualities will have no meaning. On the other hand, if we think that qualities only are real then we have to explain the fact of their unity. But a basic problem arises here. If the term quality is meaningful only in relation to a substance, and if we cannot assert the existence of a substance without qualities then we should not try to understand the reality in terms of substance and qualities. If we think that qualities cannot exist without a substance and a substance cannot be known to exist without qualities then we should not think in terms of substance and qualities to understand the nature of reality.

The problem of substance becomes further complicated when we try to understand non-material or non-physical reality like mind or consciousness. Is it meaningful to think of mind or self in terms of substance and qualities? What is the nature of relationship between body and mind or body and self if we think that both are real? Can we adopt the model of substance and qualities to understand the nature of relationship between body and mind or body and self? These problems attract our attention when we discuss the nature of reality.[4]

Trying to understand the reality in terms of substance and qualities is to an extent meaningful only with regard to physical realm of the world as every material object possesses certain qualities which distinguish it from other objects. But how to understand in terms of substance and qualities the reality of mind

---

4. See chapter on *Brahman*, and also the chapter on Spirit.

or consciousness? Can we meaningfully understand the relationship between mind and its various acts in terms of the logic of substance and qualities? Is the logic of substance meaningful to understand non-physical reality, like mind or consciousness? Can we say that the mind or consciousness is a substance and the various mental acts such as thinking, understanding, etc. are its attributes or qualities? If mind is to be viewed as substance and the acts of thinking, etc. are to be viewed as its qualities or attributes the problem of explaining the relationship between the mind and the various mental acts will arise. If the non-physical acts like thinking, understanding, etc. are to be viewed as qualities of a substance called mind or self we have to understand the nature of mind and its relation to acts like thinking. In other worlds, the problem is how to understand the reality of mind, and the manner in which it is related to the acts like thinking. However, we have to admit that in the case of mind some sort of freedom is possible to it in relation to its acts. The functions or acts of mind are not mechanical or automatic. If the mind cannot under certain circumstances act freely it at least can resist them or be indifferent to them. And if we cannot think of freedom of mind then we cannot understand the meaning of freedom as freedom is meaningful only in relation to human mind. Even for the sake of argument, if we think of mind as a substance and its functions as the qualities, for they depend upon mind for their existence, then we have to admit that mind as a substance will have no freedom with regard to its qualities. Mind has to own or possess them, which is not however the case. It is only the physical substances that are determined by their qualities as the freedom one can have in his mental life is not possible in his physical life.

So far we have been trying to understand the problems involved in viewing the reality as a substance, and the problems that arise in understanding its relation to the qualities. Can we think of the reality that is the explanation of the world as a substance, and the world with all its diversity as its attribute, and what could be the nature of that substance? How to understand the nature of the substance, or how to determine whether the substance is physical or spiritual in nature? These problems will engage our attention in the coming chapters.

3

Brahman

THE problem of this chapter is to discuss the nature of ultimate reality, the explanation for the existence of the world. We prefer the Indian term *Brahman* to indicate the ultimate reality. *Brahman* is used in the Vedāntic tradition to mean what is ultimately real, and is regarded as the reason for the existence of the world. We find different conceptions of *Brahman* as there are different systems of Vedānta philosophy.

However, they all prefer the same term *Brahman* to mean what is ultimately real though they differ significantly in their understanding of its nature as well as its relation to the world of empirical experience. We prefer the term *Brahman* to other terms, like substance or Being, as it helps in understanding the problem of what is ultimately real, according to the Indian philosophical tradition. *Brahman* does not carry with it the same meaning as that of substance or Being though they are all conceived to explain the existence of the world. Starting with the Veda, we find a continuous tradition in which attempts are made to understand *Brahman* and its nature. But no one view or understanding of *Brahman* has been recognized as final or conclusive. However, the quest to know or understand *Brahman* and its nature continues as the quest to know or understand *Brahman* is itself a philosophically meaningful activity. In trying to understand *Brahman* many have taken the help of the tradition as it helps in understanding the depth and complexity of the problem. The fact that the various attempts to understand *Brahman* have not led to any definite conclusion about *Brahman* and its nature may make one feel or realize the futility of the whole exercise. Nevertheless, an attempt to understand *Brahman* philosophically helps one in understanding his own existence, and also in clearing the mind of the various dogmas from which it suffers.

All the conceptions of *Brahman*, which we find in the Indian philosophical tradition, particularly in the tradition of Vedānta, are based on or inspired by the tradition though reasoning has played a significant role in their formation. The Upaniṣads, the basic texts of Vedānta, are the primary source of our understanding *Brahman*, and they are not revelation (Śruti) in the sense the Vedic-Saṁhitās are.[1] But, as the Upaniṣads form part of the Vedic literature they also in a technical sense form part of Śruti. However, we find in the Upaniṣads a free and fair discussion or debate on all problems of philosophy, particularly on problems related to metaphysics or ontology, and no attempt is made in the Upaniṣads to restrain or hinder free discussion on *Brahman* and its nature. Dialogue is a favoured mode of reasoning or argumentation in the Upaniṣads. However, one important thing we should always keep in mind while trying to understand the Upaniṣads is that they are mainly pedagogic in character. Their intention is to teach or instruct those who are interested or eager to understand *Brahman* and its nature. In the context of the Upaniṣads, teaching

---

1. The Vedic Saṁhitās are collections of prayers and praises addressed to various Vedic deities, either individually or collectively, and are an expression of divinely inspired devotion (*Brahma*). In a few hymns of the Veda we find speculation regarding the origin and existence of the world, and all such hymns are highly sceptical in their tone and tenor. In the Upaniṣads we do not find prayers or praises addressed to any deity. They mostly contain dialogues and debates concerning metaphysical problems, especially related to *Brahman* and self (*ātman*) of man, and the discussions are completely free from any doctrinal bias as the Upaniṣads do not try to endorse any one view on any problem. The debates are truly philosophical. They are free and critical. However, we find in the Upaniṣads some highly valuable insights regarding the nature and meaning of human reality as well as its significance in knowing or understanding *Brahman* and its nature.

does not mean imparting a doctrine on *Brahman*, but to make the student understand the problem for himself as otherwise the student will not be benefited by the instruction on *Brahman*, as *Brahman* is not a matter of faith, but what exists objectively. The teachers of the Upaniṣads who are skilled in imparting knowledge adopt different means or ways of teaching abstract metaphysical problems, especially the problems related to ontology, to the students who are eager to understand them. We find in the Upaniṣads different teachers adopting different methods of teaching. However, analysis is one of the most favoured methods adopted by the teachers of the Upaniṣads. It is employed to make one understand the basic problems of Vedānta, like the nature of consciousness, the nature of self (*ātman*) and *Brahman*. One more important thing we have to remember in trying to understand the Upaniṣads is that the methods or examples or analogies that are chosen as aids to teaching are in accordance with the requirements of teaching, like the level of the student, and the creative ability of the teacher. The persons involved either in teaching or in discussions or in dialogues are not seers or sages, but are philosophers interested in discussing and understanding philosophical problems, particularly metaphysical or ontological problems. They seldom resort to any external authority in trying to understand the problems related to *Brahman*. In other words, we do not find in the Upaniṣads any authoritarian or dogmatic approach to the problem of *Brahman*. The discussions and dialogues are mostly open, and the participants are free to raise in a debate or discussion most critical questions, which are seen as painful or inconvenient as an arrow.[2] However, the philosophers who tried to develop the philosophy of the Upaniṣads, by way of interpreting them, are the first to accept the Upaniṣadic statements as having authority in understanding the problems discussed in the Upaniṣads. The statements of the Upaniṣads are given the authority of scriptures. However, as there are several and even

2. *Bṛhadāraṇyaka Upaniṣad*, 3.8.2.

conflicting views in the Upaniṣads on any metaphysical problem, and as no view or position is endorsed by the Upaniṣads the interpreters find it difficult to depend simply on the Upaniṣadic statements either in supporting or justifying or in arguing against any metaphysical position or view. Therefore, they rely on reason either in defending or justifying their views or positions or in attacking or criticizing the rival views and positions. But generally speaking, we find in the Upaniṣads different views on various metaphysical problems which are not consistent with each other. In other words, we do not find in the Upaniṣads any attempt to impart a doctrine either on *Brahman* or on *Ātman*, or to demolish certain other doctrines. Thus the Upaniṣads are least dogmatic in their approach to any philosophical problem, and that is the reason why philosophers find it difficult to develop a consistent or coherent system of Upaniṣadic philosophy. The views and arguments expressed by several thinkers, which do not agree with each other, find their place in the Upaniṣads. Therefore, all that is said in the Upaniṣads need not be taken as reflecting the philosophy of the Upaniṣads. The Upaniṣads have neither rejected nor endorsed any view or position. They are philosophical texts in which we find the wisdom of several thinkers or philosophers collected and handed over to future generations. The Upaniṣadic approach to the problem of *Brahman* is philosophically significant as all the Upaniṣadic dialogues and debates in which the problem of *Brahman* is discussed are not doctrinal.[3] The Upaniṣads are not intended to teach a doctrine on *Brahman* which is to be accepted on faith. We are to study them, reflect upon them and try to understand their meaning critically and objectively if we are to be benefited by them. In other words, the Upaniṣads are open in their approach.

The Upaniṣadic quest to know or understand that by knowing or understanding which all that is there is known is truly

3. Ibid., 2.1.1-20; 2.4.1-5; 3.3.1-2; 3.5.1; 3.6.1; *Chāndogya Upaniṣad*, the whole of chapter 6.

philosophical in spirit. However, we do not come across in the Upaniṣads the reasoning process involved in understanding a problem and its possible solution as it would be cumbersome to preserve in an oral tradition all the details. Nevertheless, in many cases the process is indicated. Therefore, the freedom to understand and interpret the philosophy of the Upaniṣads is there in the Upaniṣads themselves. Even in the Vedic Saṁhitās freedom to enquire and question is not denied in all matters concerning metaphysics. As most of the hymns of the Saṁhitās are prayers or praises addressed to the deities there is nothing to be critical about them. But when it comes to know or understand the existence and nature of what is ultimately real we find freedom which often leads to scepticism. Scepticism is generally the tone of the hymns in which the basic metaphysical problems are discussed, and reflected upon.[4] However, in the Upaniṣads we also find a quest to know *Brahman* which is direct and immediate, or *Brahman* which we can know or intuit directly and immediately. The reality that is the source as well as the substance of the world we experience must itself be real. *Brahman* that is "direct and immediate" is not the same as the *Brahman* of speculative metaphysics. *Brahman* of metaphysics is meant to explain the existence of the world, and is therefore defined and re-defined till the concept of *Brahman* is found adequate or sufficient to explain the existence of the world. But *Brahman* that is known directly and immediately is not a postulate meant to explain the world, but is seen as being present in all that is there.[5]

Thus we find in the Upaniṣads two different ways of understanding *Brahman*. According to one way of understanding, *Brahman* is viewed as the cause of the world, and therefore its existence and nature are sought to be known inferentially on the basis of the world of empirical experience. According to the other

---

4. *Ṛgveda Saṁhitā*, Nāsadīya Sūkta, 1.164.
5. *Bṛhādaraṇyaka Upaniṣad*, 3.4.1-2; 3.5.1, *Sākṣāt aparokṣāt brahma* (*Brahman* that is direct and immediate or unmediated).

way of understanding, *Brahman* is viewed as the essence as well as the inner unity of all that is there. If we think that the world of empirical experience has no independent existence or is a caused reality then we are justified in trying to know or understand its cause as it helps in understanding the world and its nature. On the other hand, our approach to *Brahman* will be significantly different if we accept that the world is all that is there as we cannot think of limits to the world, and in that case to know *Brahman* is to know that which sustains the world by being its essence. Such approach to *Brahman* also helps in understanding the reality of man as what is sufficient to explain the world of empirical experience may not be significant in knowing or understanding the reality of man. In trying to understand *Brahman* and its nature if we take into consideration the world of empirical experience our understanding of *Brahman* will be significantly different from our understanding of *Brahman* in which we take into consideration not only the world of empirical experience but also the reality of man. Can we say that the reality which is sufficient to explain the existence of the world is equally sufficient to explain the reality of man, or the reality that is adequate to understand and explain human reality is sufficient to understand and explain the reality of the world? Can we say that to understand the reality of man we have to understand the reality of the world, or to understand the world we have to understand the reality of man? Is it relevant to view man and understand his reality in relation to the world, or to understand the reality of the world we have to understand it in relation to man? Are they integral to each other? Can we say that our understanding of the world is complete and comprehensive without an understanding human reality, and vice versa? In other words, can we say that what is sufficient to explain the world may not be so to explain the reality of man, though the reality of man is really significant in knowing or understanding the world. What is man's place in the world, and how far his reality is significant in understanding the reality of the world? Why in the first place we think that the reality of man is something unique and different from or unrelated to the reality of the world? Are they two really different realities so that the reality of one is not significant in understanding the reality of the other?

Now, it is man who tries to understand the reality of the world as well as his own reality, and in doing so he thinks of himself as superior to and distinct from the world he tries to understand. The world is an object of his experience, knowledge and enjoyment. And man regards the world as the source of fulfilment of his needs and desires, but not as the source of fulfilment of his life and existence. He thinks that the source of fulfilment of his life or existence is not the world of empirical experience, and he looks to a reality which is other than the world for the fulfilment of his existence. Thus man's attitude towards the world is either to view it as an object of enjoyment or as something from which he has to detach or withdraw himself because he sees in it a source of hindrance or obstruction for the fulfilment of his existence. In either sense man's attitude towards the world is not conducive to an objective or dispassionate understanding of the world and its nature. As a knower to whom the world is given as an object of experience and knowledge, man can distinguish himself from the world which makes him think that his reality is different from that of the world, and therefore one and the same reality cannot be the explanation of both. While he is a knower the world is always an object to him. Thus the important reason why man thinks of himself as distinct from the world is the reality of his self. Man finds within himself the presence or reality of self which seems to have no affinity to the world of empirical experience. And because of the presence of self in him man thinks that he does not wholly belong to the world. As man thinks that the reality of self is different from or even alien to the world of empirical experience it cannot be of any help in understanding the reality of the world. Likewise, he thinks that his understanding of the world cannot help him in understanding the reality of self. They are viewed as two independent realities, and therefore, the understanding of one cannot help in understanding the other. And if we think we are justified in accepting such a position there is no reason why we have to take into consideration the reality of man in understanding the reality of the world, or the reality of the world in understanding the reality of self. One cannot be explained in terms of the other, and more importantly, both cannot be explained in terms of the same reality. We have then to admit two independent realities, one to explain the world and the other to explain human reality or self. As the reality of man is fundamentally different from the reality of the world both cannot have their explanation in one and the same reality.

But if we understand by world all that is an object of experience or knowledge to man then it is meaningful to explain its existence in terms of a single reality, and if we accept the definition of matter as that which is an object of knowledge or enjoyment then matter can be the explanation of the world of empirical experience. According to this view, except the reality of man, everything can be explained in terms of matter, or in terms of ordinary language, except the reality of self, everything is a manifestation of matter. On the other hand, if we understand by world all that is there the problem of explaining the reality of man in terms of the reality which is sufficient to explain the world of empirical experience arises. By human reality we mean his spiritual being as well as his physical or bodily existence, and both are integral to human reality as man is not complete without one or the other. Here we have to understand whether the self of man and his body represent two independent realities which somehow are united or integrated in human reality. Although man is a unity of both matter and spirit the problem of their co-existence arises when we think that one is opposed to the other. In the case of man the opposition is clear and obvious as man is both an observer and the observed or a subject and an object. Not only the physical world is an object of experience and understanding to man, but his own reality, that is, his physical life is an object of knowledge and understanding to man. Man knows himself, and tries to understand his own reality, just as he tries to understand the reality of the world. He can have an understanding of himself as he can make himself an object of his understanding. He can distinguish or detach himself, at least in understanding, from his body and mind, and observe them and their functions as he observes the world. However, the self of man, the reason for his subjectivity, can know itself as different from the physical reality of man. The ability to distinguish or detach oneself from his body and mind, and view them as objects of knowledge is the unique characteristic of man, and because of such ability man thinks of himself as a unity of two realities of matter and spirit. However, they cannot be separated in the life of man though they can be distinguished, and they are so united or integrated in the life of man one cannot exist without the other. Then what gives man a sense of unity, or how to understand and explain the relationship between the body and self or spirit in man. Are they two independent realities radically different from each other, but somehow live together in the person of man? Or are they two sides or aspects of the same reality that is man? If they are two aspects of man then what would be the nature of man which has two opposing principles as his nature?

Here the basic problem is how far are we justified in trying to understand man as something more than his body and mind? If man is more than his body and mind in what way the body and mind are related to him as a person? Can we say, on the other hand, that the concept of man as something more than his body and mind is just an illusion? If we accept the view that man is more than his body and mind we have to explain the manner in which man, as a person, is related to his body and mind as it will have a bearing on the larger problem of the relationship between matter and spirit or consciousness. It is in man we find that matter and spirit or body and consciousness are united. Though we can find pure matter we do not find anywhere pure or disembodied spirit or consciousness. Even in the reality of man we find them inseparably related. However, the way we understand the problem of relationship between body and mind or consciousness in man will help us in understanding the problem of relationship between *Brahman* and world. We may here consider certain examples to understand the problem more clearly as the examples are taken from outside the human realm. Let us consider the example of a tree.[6] In the process of its growth a tree gives rise to flowers and fruits. The flower, its beauty and fragrance, the fruit, its flavour and other qualities like taste, etc. have no similarity to the trunk or roots or other parts of the tree, as the latter do not share the characteristic qualities of flower and fruit. Similarly, the seed, the source of a tree, does not apparently have the qualities of the tree, including those of flower and fruit. Now, how are we to understand the relationship between the parts of the tree like trunk and roots and its flower and fruit. The explanation is obvious. The seed contains within itself the tree, and the tree within itself the flower and fruit though potentially, and the evolution of the seed brings forth all that it is capable of growing into, or all that is there within itself potentially. Though we do not find any likeness or similarity between the seed and the tree, and the tree and its various parts, especially its flower and fruit and their finer qualities, we accept that all these are there within the seed in a potential form or condition. Now, instead of viewing them as due to the evolution of the same seed, if we try to understand the relationship between the trunk and roots of the tree with its flowers, fruits, flavours, and fragrance which are in no way similar to each other we find it difficult to relate them. The beauty of the flower and the taste of the fruit are not to be found in other parts of the tree. Apparently they are unrelated though they are related in a deeper sense. They are not related as

6. *Chāndogya Upaniṣad*, 6.11.1-2.

they are not similar to each other, but are related as they belong to the same tree, and live the same life. This is only an example taken from a different realm, and cannot therefore be taken literally to understand the relationship between human body and mind. One more example taken from the human realm may help us in understanding the problem. What kind of relation we can think of between the human mind and its varied creations? The human creativity and the varied forms of its creation or expression are in a way related which cannot be compared with the relationships we find among physical objects. Even among some of the physical objects we find it difficult to understand and determine the nature of relationship. For instance, how to determine the relationship between the sun and sunshine, lamp and its light, or a gem and its lustre? We think that the relationship between a substance and its qualities is one of dependence as the qualities cannot exist by themselves. The qualities subsist in something which we call substance. But what is the nature of substance apart from or without the qualities is a problem. We cannot think of substance without qualities as we cannot think of qualities independently of a substance. A substance may acquire certain qualities and characteristics, but certain qualities are intrinsic to it. We cannot therefore think of a substance without qualities. Can we now say that the sun is the substance and light or shining is its intrinsic quality, or lamp is the substance and light is its intrinsic quality? We make a distinction between the sun and sunlight or the lamp and light because we employ different words to indicate them. But how can we decide whether they are really related? For instance, we can change some of the qualities of an object. Some qualities like the colour can be added and some other qualities can be taken away from the substance. And before we add a quality, like colour, to an object we can see the quality and the object separately. In other words, we can see the colour and object separately before they are related. Therefore there is no problem in understanding the relation between them as we know the object and the quality independently before they are related. And it is the minimum requirement to establish a relationship between two things. However, this is true with regard to acquired or secondary qualities only. Can we say the same thing with regard to primary or intrinsic qualities? Can we think of the sun without sunshine, or a gem without its lustre, or fire without burning so that we can think of their being related? And when we cannot think of two things independently of each other there is no justification in trying to view them as two, and then trying to relate them. When we cannot think of fire without heat, or the sun without light, it is redundant to think of two things of fire and heat or sun and light, and then trying to relate them. In reality they are not two things which are to be related, or there is no relationship between them for they are not different. Though fire and heat may appear to mean two things in reality one is not meaningful without the other. We cannot think of fire without heat or burning and burning without fire, or the sun without light.

We have tried to understand the various ways in which things can be related. But how to understand the meaning of relationship, or when we can say that things are related? Though the problem seems to be trivial it can throw light on the main problem of the relationship between *Brahman* and the world. As we have discussed earlier any type of relationship is possible between two things as one and the same thing cannot be related to itself. However, a thing can be related to itself in the sense that the different modes of its existence can be related to each other. The same person can be related to himself in terms of the modes of his existence, or in terms of the various functions he performs, either in family or in society. For example, a person can be differentiated on the basis of the forms of his existence or in terms of the functions he performs, and in terms of such differences he can be related to himself. In other words, the relations are established between the various forms or functions of a person though as a person he is one, and cannot therefore be related to himself.

Similarly the same substance can be differentiated in terms of its forms which can be related to each other in terms of the qualities they acquire. Gold in one form of its existence can be differentiated and related to the other forms of its existence? In one form of its existence gold may acquire certain qualities which it may not have in other forms of its existence. Thus the same thing can be related to itself in terms of its forms or functions. But what kind of relationship we can think of between gold and the various forms of its existence? It cannot be one of cause and effect nor is it a case of evolution. Let us consider another example. For instance, we accept that matter is the reality of the physical world, or the reality of things and phenomena we empirically experience, which differ significantly among themselves. How do we recognize matter in the diverse forms of its existence, or how do we recognize matter in all the things of the world? According to Indian materialists (Cārvākas), matter is the reality of the world, and they define matter as that which is an object of sense experience. Since spirit is not an object of sense experience it is not real as to be real it is to be an object of sense experience. Generally speaking, the Indian philosophers define matter as that which is an object of sense experience, or anything that is an object of sense experience is matter. But they have not tried to investigate as to what is actually experienced by our senses. We experience several qualities and forms but not matter as such which is supposed to be the basis or substratum of the qualities and forms. Matter is an object of understanding as without admitting its existence we cannot understand and explain the unity of a thing or an object or the physical world as such. An object or a thing is seen as one though it consists of several things, like qualities. And if we think that an object or a thing is constituted of several things, like qualities, we have to understand the reason for their unity, or what keeps them together. It is the substance which, we think, keeps the things together or united. We can understand this better if we take into consideration the organic realm, or the realm of living beings.

What keeps a tree united, or why we call a tree a tree despite the fact that it is a unity of several things like branches, leaves and flowers? These things are not joined together to form a whole as in the case of an artefact like chariot. It is the life sap that flows or runs through the tree, and sustains or keeps the tree alive and together. It pervades the whole tree, and is the life as well as the unity of the tree. We may say that the life sap of a tree is the *ātman* or self of the tree without which the tree cannot exist, and be one. Though it is not an object of sense experience it is real; it is the source of unity of the tree. Among the living beings, life pervades the whole body and sustains it, and also forms the unity of a living being. However, in the case of human beings, though life keeps a human being alive and together, it is the self (*ātman*) that is the essential characteristic of a human being, or what makes a living being a human being. What distinguishes a human being from all other living beings is the self which is more than life. To be a human being is more than to be a living being as in a human being more than life is involved which we may call the self of man. The self of man distinguishes man from all other living beings. It gives man individuality, and makes him understand himself and the world. It is basically the principle of knowledge, and makes man a knowing being, or a centre of knowledge. Knowledge in the Indian context is a wider term, and can cover or comprehend all intellectual activities of man which generate knowledge, understanding, both rational and non-rational, and all kinds of creativity which result in literature, music, etc. and in which man rejoices or delights. These are self-fulfilling activities of man. Now, man as man finds himself in all he does and knows. To be able to know, understand, critically reflect upon, imagine, etc. are all typically human characteristics or qualities, and self is seen as the centre or source of all such activities as well as their unity. Man not only tries to know or understand the world around him, but also himself.

Now, how to understand the nature of relationship between man and his self?

Our understanding of the nature of relationship between man and his self may help us in understanding the relationship between the world and *Brahman*, as human reality is the best possible analogy to understand *Brahman* and its relationship to the world of empirical experience. It is in human reality we see a clear manifestation of spirit or consciousness. In no other reality of the world we see a clear and nearly perfect manifestation of spirit. More significantly, we see in the reality of man an integration or unity of matter and spirit, though in our empirical experience we find opposition between matter and spirit. The opposition between matter and spirit is what we clearly see in a knowledge situation in which the dichotomy of subject and object is involved. An object is always an object, and a subject is always a subject, and one cannot become the other because of the opposition between them. And yet we see them integrated or united in the reality of man. Man is neither pure matter nor pure spirit. He is both, and yet he is one in the sense he is the unity of matter and spirit. He is one in whom the seeming opposition between matter and spirit is obliterated.

How to understand and explain the unity of matter and spirit in man? If they are really opposed to each other how can they be united in man or how can we explain their unity in man. In other words, if matter and spirit are opposed to each other they cannot find their unity in man. And if they are united in man then the opposition between them may not be real. Though at the level of empirical experience we find opposition between matter and spirit, in reality they may not be opposed to each other. The idea of opposition between matter and spirit is based on our empirical experience of them. The nature of matter as it is known at the empirical level, or our understanding of it at the level of empirical experience may not be its true nature. It is possible that matter is not really different from spirit or consciousness ultimately. As we have discussed in the chapter on Matter, philosophical understanding of matter is different from its popular conception.

And our understanding of matter changes significantly as we come to know and understand the varied and diverse manifestations of matter. All the manifestations of matter do not show the same characteristic, or the nature of matter does not seem to be homogeneous if we try to understand the nature of matter on the basis of its varied and diverse manifestations. And if we accept the Indian view that mind and its creations are also physical and are the manifestation of matter, then our understanding of matter will be significantly different from the popular conception of it as something static and opposed to all that is good and noble. Human mind is nearer to spirit, and its creativity is as good as an expression of spirit. The music, literature, philosophy and all such creative expressions of man are basically expressions or creations of human mind though it is a manifestation of matter, and most of the creations of mind, like music and literature, are ends in themselves. They do not bind man, or hamper the expression of his spirit. Most of the spiritual things are in reality the creations or expressions of human mind, according to Indian philosophy. Therefore, mind is neither pure matter nor pure spirit. It is in between the body and self, and is seen to possess the qualities of both. Because of its subtlety and transparent character there is confusion between mind and spirit, and many people therefore identify mind with spirit. The reason for such confusion is the nature of mind. According to Vedānta, because of its transparent character, which can be improved and made like spirit (*śuddha sattva*), the nature of the spirit is reflected in mind, and that leads to the confusion between mind and spirit.[7] Because of its very subtle nature mind is known and identified in terms of its functions like thinking, understanding, etc. However, as mind is constituted of finest matter it is helpful in understanding the nature of matter than most of the manifestations of matter. Thus our understanding of matter differs significantly depending upon our attitude

---

7. In Sāṁkhya as well as in Vedānta mind is regarded as physical, or as a subtle form of matter.

towards matter as well as the evidence we take into consideration in understanding its nature. However, the reason why we see opposition between matter and spirit, which seems to be meaningful and real at the level of empirical experience, is because of the fact that we attach two significantly different values to them. Matter as it manifests itself in the form of human body, including mind, is seen as a source of misery and suffering, or the main reason for all that is evil in man, whereas the spirit is seen as the source of all that is good and noble. While matter is mortal, limited and imperfect, the spirit is regarded as immortal and perfect. Human perfection and glory are somehow thwarted by his body and mind which man has to overcome or conquer to attain real perfection which is spiritual. The spirit is somehow trapped within the body which is matter, the reason for his suffering and misery. Because of such an attitude towards matter we find it difficult to understand and appreciate the nature of matter dispassionately or objectively, and as a result we find opposition between matter and spirit. We therefore think that both matter and spirit cannot co-exist or be united, and to the extent the philosophers are influenced by the different values attached to the matter and spirit their understanding of matter cannot be objective. Thus because of our attitude towards matter most of us think that to know man and his reality is to know or realize his self which is not his body and mind.

Now, let us try to analyse and understand the reality of self. Is it an independent reality existing in the human body, but is not integral to it? The fact that the self can be distinguished from the body and mind does not mean that it has a reality different from that of body or mind. The self is known as the seat or centre of consciousness, and the nature of consciousness is such that it cannot be attributed to body or mind as they are known to self as objects of knowledge. However, the self in man is not pure consciousness, and has no independent reality as it is known to exist in relation to human body. The self reveals itself in and through the functions of mind, and in the absence of such functions it is also not known to exist. In the classical Indian tradition, which includes the Upaniṣads, self is seen as the essence (*ātman*) of a thing or a phenomenon.[8] *Ātman* (self) is that because of which a thing or a phenomenon is identified and defined. For instance, burning is the essence of fire as without the capacity to burn we cannot know fire and identify it. And fire may acquire certain qualities in relation to the things it burns. At the empirical level we know fire when it burns something, but not fire as such. Burning requires, besides fire, something to be burnt. Thus in every instance of fire we see fire plus something which it burns. In the Indian philosophical tradition, especially in the Vedānta, consciousness is known as the essence (*ātman*) or self of man which gives him his identity, and distinguishes him from other living beings. Man is known and identified in terms of consciousness which is his essence (*ātman*) or self.[9] The self is known or regarded as the essence of man, or it is the defining characteristic of man. Therefore, in identifying consciousness as the essence or self of man the other things or aspects of man are not separated from his essence. As the essential reality or essence (*ātman*) of man consciousness is not different from man or his body and mind. It is integral to the reality of man, but not an independent reality living in him. It can only be distinguished from the other aspects of man, but not separated. It is not alien to the reality of man as it is integral to his reality. It is the essence or the defining characteristic of man in terms of which man is known and identified. Essence of man means what is essential to be a human being, but not something which exists in man independently of his body and mind. The self as the essential reality of man is integral to the reality of man, as otherwise it cannot be the essence of man. The essence of a thing is intrinsic to the thing, but not something different from or other than the thing. Thus nowhere in the classical Indian tradition *ātman* is

8. *Bṛhadāraṇyaka Upaniṣad*, 3.7.3-23; *Chāndogya Upaniṣad*, 6.9-10.
9. *Chāndogya Upaniṣad*, 6.9.10.

exclusively identified with the essence of a human being. *Brahman* forms the essence (*ātman*) of all that is there, including man, and consciousness is identified as the essence (*ātman*) of man, as burning is the essence of fire. Then why we think in terms of opposition between self and body? The opposition is meaningful only at the level of empirical experience in which we distinguish self from the body and mind in terms of values we attach to them. However, without body and mind the self has no meaning, or we cannot think of it or know it or understand its nature.

But, how to understand the fact that self is always a subject but not the object of knowledge or understanding? Let us try to understand in what sense we can understand the distinction between subject and object in relation to human body and self. Is the relationship between human body and self similar to the one in which man is the subject and the world around him is the object? Let us understand the situations in which man knows himself as the subject. For instance, man knows that he is in the world, and also knows that he is not the world. Is the self-knowledge of man like that of his knowledge of the world? Man knows that he is in a room, and also knows that he is not the room. While in the case of the world man cannot come out of the world or separate himself from the world though he knows that he is not the world, in the case of room he can separate himself from the room, and can live without the room. Can we say that the self of man is in his body, just as he is in a room or the world? If these situations are similar then the self of man can separate itself from the body of man, and live without it which, however, is not the case. Man cannot even imagine the state of self's disembodied existence. Is man's knowledge of himself similar to his knowledge of the world or of the room? Man's knowledge of the world has a content which he can communicate to others. If self is consciousness and is not related to his body and mind then the knowledge of self should have no content, and cannot therefore be communicated. The fact that consciousness is not an object of knowledge to others is no reason to deny self-knowledge to man. When man knows that he is a conscious being, as he can know and understand things other than himself, he comes to know the meaning of consciousness. At least he knows that consciousness is behind his senses and mind, or inspires them in knowing and understanding things, as we know electricity as that which is the source of illumination in a lamp. Man knows consciousness as that because of which his senses and mind are able to know and understand things. Our knowledge of consciousness is not because of our effort to know it but because of the nature of consciousness which is self-revealing. Man knows that he exists not because he knows his existence in the way he knows things other than himself but because of the self-revealing character of consciousness. Therefore, consciousness need not become an object to itself in knowing itself. However, in knowing himself as one who knows, thinks and understands, human mind is involved just as his senses are involved in knowing himself as one who perceives things. Therefore without the involvement of his body and mind man cannot know himself or his self which is involved in all that he knows and understands. In this process we cannot say that senses and mind are used as instruments by the self as self cannot know things without the senses and the mind. It sees, hears, knows, thinks and understands by being the essence or the very capacity of the senses and the mind, as consciousness cannot stop itself from being aware of things. It is the very nature of consciousness to be aware of things that come into contact with it. Thus the self is not the essence of any one part of man. It is the essence of man in the sense that it is not different from his body and mind. It is by being within the senses and mind as their essence or their capacity, consciousness helps them in perceiving, knowing, thinking and understanding things. It is by being within the senses the self perceives, and by being within the mind it knows, thinks and understand things, and in perceiving or knowing things it knows itself. Thus as the essence of man the self has no independent existence, or it has no reality of its own. It is not different from man or his mind or his senses, just as man is not different from his body and mind. Man is one as his body, mind and self are not different from himself.

The self as the essence or the essential reality of man is meaningful only in understanding the reality of man. As the essence of man self is not different from him or his reality. The essence of a thing or a phenomenon is not separate from the thing or the phenomenon, and if it is different or can be separated from the thing or phenomenon it cannot be their essence. If self or consciousness is different or separate from man it cannot be the essence or self of man, and therefore in knowing himself man knows himself as the self which is the essential aspect of his reality. Thus if we understand by self, the essence (*ātman*) of man, there can be no opposition between the self and body because they are not really different. And therefore in knowing itself self knows itself as the essence of man but not as different from man, just as in knowing *Brahman* we know all that is there, as *Brahman* is the essence (*ātman*) of all that is there. The above analysis should not be misconstrued to mean that matter is the cause of consciousness or consciousness is the cause of matter or the human body. In its true nature matter is not different from consciousness because consciousness is the essence or the true or real nature of matter or the world of our empirical experience. Therefore, in knowing the world of empirical experience truly or in its real nature we know *Brahman*. The world and *Brahman* are not therefore related as they are not different. However, we discuss this more fully in the next chapter.

But how to understand the relationship between body and spirit or self, and the opposition between them which is experienced at the empirical level? Though spirit does not share any of the characteristics of the body they are together or co-exist in the reality of man. How is it then possible for them to live together or be united or integrated? We find several explanations within the Indian philosophical tradition about the nature of their relationship. However, most of the people find it difficult to establish any real relationship between them, and the reasons are mainly religious. If the spirit is really related to the body, or if they are really united or integrated in man then the spirit cannot hope to become free from the limitations of the body. Therefore the only way to explain their living together in a person is to view self as being entrapped in the body. The spirit finds itself entrapped in a body which it considers as bondage, and therefore tries to escape itself from the body. But philosophically speaking the relationship between a physical reality and a spiritual reality poses several problems which are highly significant to understand the problem of ultimate reality and its nature. From the empirical point of view, the body and spirit are two different realities which are opposed to each other. The spirit is a conscious principle, and is known as the subject to which the body and mind are objects of knowledge. But spirit is not an object of knowledge to any other reality. Considering the opposition between the two many think that they are two different realities which somehow co-exist and are united in man. But man is a whole, and he does not experience any gulf between his body and spirit in real life. Man does not know himself as a combination of two distinct or different realities. He sees himself as one, and acts as one. He, however, experiences tension between his spirit and body which is mostly due to his cultural or religious beliefs. However, if the body and spirit are really opposed to each other, as we empirically think, we cannot explain the fact that they are together in man. How could they co-exist or live together if they are really opposed to each other in their natures? They cannot be related in any manner because of the opposition. But how to understand and explain the fact of their co-existence or unity? How to understand the co-existence of two things or realities which are opposed to each other in their natures? Can we say that the spirit is the essence and the body is its outer manifestation? But we have to remember that to be really related they must have independent existence or be able to exist independently of each other. This is, however, not the case with spirit and body as we do not find disembodied spirit, and a person without spirit or self.

If we think that spirit is the essence and the body its manifestation then the problem of explaining their natures which are opposed to each other will arise. How two things which are opposed to each other can be related as essence and manifestation? Water cannot be the essence of fire or fire the essence of water. But we can understand the meaning of essence differently. Essence is not different from the other aspects of the reality of which it is the essence as it is present in all the aspects; it sustains them and forms their unity. Without the essence a thing cannot sustain itself. Essence is also known as that which gives identity to a thing, as the thing is known and identified in terms of its essence. In the classical Indian tradition the word *ātman* is used to mean the essence in the above sense. It is said that *Brahman* or the ultimate reality is the *atman* of all that is there. How we come to know the essence of a thing? These problems will engage our attention when we discuss the nature of *Brahman*. But one thing is clear that every reality is known and identified in terms of its essence, and therefore essence will have no meaning independently of a thing or a phenomenon. Essence is what is essential to a thing or a reality. We have to discuss or at least point out here the possible relationship between self and man. It is one thing to understand or know the nature of relationship between two material realities, and the relationship between matter and spirit. But quite distinct from the two types of relationships we have to understand the nature of relationship between self and its manifestations or expressions. How to explain the relationship between self and its manifestations like knowing and seeing? How to understand the relation between creativity and its creations or expressions? We can here think of an example which may help in understanding the problem. A tree is pervaded by its essence, the sap, that runs through the tree, and sustains it though it cannot be experienced from outside. Now the tree consists of so many things like trunk, bark, branches, leaves, flowers, fruits, etc. and all these do not have much similarity among themselves. For instance, the fragrance and beauty of a flower have no similarity with the trunk and bark of the tree, but yet both are integral to the tree, and are sustained by the same essence. Thus the essence and the other aspects of a thing or reality are not really different so that they can be related.

4

Matter

MATTER as we empirically know it is not a homogeneous reality having a definite or clearly definable nature. In the Indian philosophical tradition we find several views about matter. While most of the philosophers understand by matter the five basic elements of earth, water, fire, air and space, that constitute the world, some regard even mind as a subtle form of matter. According to Jaina philosophers, *karma* (action) as well as its influence upon man are basically physical in nature.[1] But almost all the philosophers are of the view that matter is atomic in structure as any material object can be analysed into atoms, the simple parts of matter. However, there is no single definition of matter though it is known to all. We find several definitions of it, like it occupies space or has extension, or is analysable, or is an object of sense experience. However, in all these definitions no attempt is made to say anything about the real nature or essence of matter. We think of several things when we try to understand the nature of matter, like a hard rock or a piece of iron, flowing water, burning fire, blowing wind, a tender flower and its beauty and fragrance. According to Indian philosophy, even mind and its creations are physical in nature. The tender emotions and feelings are also the manifestations of matter, or they are physical.

---

1. *Indian Philosophy*, vol. I, S. Radhakrishnan, p. 319. *Karma* according to the Jainas is of material nature (*paudgalika*). Only thus can the Jainas conceive that thoughts and ideas affect our character and create or modify the tendencies of our souls. The kind of matter fit to manifest *karma* fills all cosmic space. The soul by its commerce with the outer world becomes literally penetrated with the particles of subtle matter.

Matter in the form of food can nourish and sustain life, and in the form of beauty can attract and entice man, and in terms of its varied possibilities can enrich the world of human experience. It can destroy life in the form of fire, and can sustain it as well in the form of warmth that is essential for the growth, survival and sustenance of life. Matter in the varied forms of its manifestation like fire, water, earth, etc. is present everywhere. The Sāṁkhya conception of matter is so rich, beautiful, tender and creative that it is viewed as the explanation of all that is there with the exception of consciousness. It is the source of enjoyment as well as bondage, and it even helps indirectly man's liberation from itself.[2] It is dynamic, and in terms of its inner dynamism it is the source of the world of multiplicity which we all experience and enjoy. In its manifestation as mind it is the source of restlessness in man as well as the source of tranquillity and peace. Dynamism and rest are the forms of its manifestation as mind. For instance, if we take the example of tree, it means and includes its roots, trunk, bark, branches, flowers, their fragrance as well as their beauty. We cannot say that the trunk only, the most tangible part of the tree, is the tree, but not the fragrance and beauty of its flower. All are manifestations of the same reality, and therefore, we have no justification in trying to understand the reality of a tree or a seed in terms of some of its most tangible forms of manifestation.

Even according to physics, matter is not what we mean by it ordinarily, that is something hard, solid and tangible. The fact that matter and energy are convertible terms, and the fact that light also is a form of matter is something which we ordinarily cannot understand and appreciate. It is matter that is the source of all energy, including mental or intellectual energy, or it is energy itself but appearing as stable or solid. The creative energy of human mind is also a form of matter. Except consciousness, which in its nature is seen as opposed to matter, everything is matter or the

2. *Sāṁkhya Kārikā*, vv. 55 and 56. There is nothing more tender (*sukumaratararam*) than *prakṛti* in my view.

varied forms of its manifestation. Human mind in its creativity manifests or expresses itself in so rich and varied forms it is difficult to determine its nature or essence. In a human being the hair and nails are organic and living, but if we define life as that which can feel or experience pain and pleasure, nails and hair are not to be regarded as living, for there is absence of pain in them. Nevertheless, they are living as they manifest some of the characteristics of life, like growth. Human brain, the seat of human mind, and human heart, the seat of emotions and feelings, are material in nature as they are influenced by the conditions of human body. The fragrance and beauty of a flower are physical, and what we find in them cannot be found in the other forms of matter. Also the way they affect us is different from the ways in which other manifestations of matter affect us. Let us consider the example of music, a subtle form of matter. Its impact on man or the way it affects man is almost spiritual, and yet it is a manifestation of matter; it is basically sound. Thus if we understand the varied forms of manifestation of matter it is really difficult to understand and appreciate the meaning or essence of matter. The various ways in which matter influences or affects man also helps us in understanding the richness of matter. It is so rich and varied in the forms of its manifestation it defies all our efforts to determine its nature. The way the destruction caused by an atom bomb affects man is completely different from the way in which music or literature or the beauty of a flower or the serenity of nature influences man. While nature in some of its aspects is mechanical or is amenable to mechanical laws, in some other aspects nature is inspiring and creative. Human creativity or the creativity of human mind defies all our attempts to determine its nature. Thus matter can be both passive and dynamic, awful and peaceful, mechanical and creative. And in a sense it is the source of all emotions and feelings.

However, the only reality the philosophers find it difficult to understand and explain in terms of matter is consciousness. The basic characteristic of matter, which is common to all the forms of its manifestation, is the fact of its being an object of knowledge or experience. In general terms, anything that can be an object of knowledge or experience is matter, and that which knows or experiences is consciousness. The duality of knower and known, which is involved in all that we know and experience, is the basic characteristic of human experience and knowledge, as in the absence of any one of them knowledge or experience is not possible. The duality of knower and known or the subject and object is involved in all that we know and experience, and as far as empirical experience is concerned this duality cannot be overcome or transcended. In the absence of consciousness there can be no knowledge or experience of anything, and similarly in the absence of an object, whatever may be its nature, there can be no experience. Even to think or imagine about the world that is devoid of consciousness is possible only when there is a conscious being to whom such thinking or imagination is possible, as well as significant. Of course, this is purely a trivial problem. But the fact is the world of our empirical experience involves the duality of knower and known, and in the absence of such duality there can be no knowledge or experience. Now, the important problem is whether matter can be the source or explanation of consciousness. Is it possible for matter to evolve itself into consciousness, or can we think of consciousness as a form of manifestation of matter? Can we say that somehow matter is the source of consciousness, because we cannot find consciousness as such or in its disembodied state? Consciousness is always found in association with matter or living beings. Can we say that matter is the ultimate reality or the primordial being, and is therefore the sole explanation for the existence of the world, including consciousness or spirit? However, no final word is said so far about the real nature of matter even by the science. Maybe the future can show that matter and spirit are not really different, or are not two things. It is equally possible to think that in future we may come to know that matter is a form of consciousness or consciousness is a mode or manifestation of matter. We are not in a position to deny any such possibility seeing how our understanding of matter changes significantly. But our concern is purely conceptual or philosophical whatever may be its worth or significance in understanding the problem.

The manifestations of matter though differ widely in terms of their forms and functions share the fundamental characteristic of matter, that is, they are objects of experience, knowledge and understanding. The light which is a manifestation of matter can illuminate objects as well as itself, but it cannot know objects or itself. Matter in any form of its manifestation is not a subject or that which knows. The various sense organs which are physical can know or perceive only when they are enlivened or inspired by consciousness. They cannot by themselves or without being enlivened by consciousness perceive anything. They have to depend upon consciousness to know or perceive. Even the mind which seems to be spiritual or conscious, and performs several functions like thinking, remembering, understanding, etc. cannot perform its functions if it is not inspired or enlivened by consciousness. We have to understand the problem whether the senses and mind by themselves or without being enlivened by consciousness can know or experience things. We discuss in a separate chapter the various arguments to show that the senses and mind are only instruments of cognition, but not the real source or explanation of cognition.[3] However, one significant argument to show that the senses and mind are only instruments of cognition is that they are material in nature; they are as physical as any part of human body. They are objects of cognition as any other part of human body. The functions of mind as well as the functions of the senses are objects of knowledge. Just as the human body is influenced by physical conditions like food and environment, the senses and mind are also influenced by physical

3 See chapters on Consciousness and Spirit.

factors like food and environment. Defective sense organs can distort our vision or perception of things, and mind if it is weak cannot perform its functions properly.

Can matter be the explanation of spirit or consciousness? How can we know whether matter is the cause or explanation of consciousness or not? If consciousness depends upon matter for its existence or if matter is the source of consciousness then we cannot think of independent existence of consciousness. Can we think of matter as the explanation of consciousness, or can we say that matter is the source of consciousness or consciousness is a form of manifestation of matter? Can matter somehow develop or evolve itself into consciousness? As pointed out earlier the manifestations of matter differ widely among themselves, and they do not have any one quality, except form, in common. Yet we regard them all as manifestations of matter because they are objects of knowledge or experience. They all belong to the realm of objects. While most of the forms of matter are not caused by any external agency but are due to inner dynamism of matter, some of the forms of manifestation are due to human agency. But matter is present in all the forms of its manifestation. How can we know whether consciousness is also a form of manifestation of matter? Is it the case that matter in its most subtle form manifests itself as consciousness, or gives rise to consciousness? If consciousness is to be a form of manifestation of matter then matter should be present in consciousness, as it is present in all the forms of its manifestation. But how to know or prove whether matter is present in consciousness or is the essence of consciousness? If consciousness is to be a form of manifestation of matter it must have some form, and be an object of knowledge as all the forms of matter have some form, and are objects of knowledge. But we cannot say that consciousness has a form though in a figurative sense it is said that it assumes the forms of objects of knowledge. In itself it has no form, and if it has a form of its own it cannot assume, as it were, the various forms of its objects. Without having a form of its own, it assumes, as it were, all the forms of matter in knowing them, just as water assumes the forms of the vessels.

Even for the sake of argument, if we assume that matter somehow becomes or is the source of consciousness then the following logical problems arise. Matter as matter cannot be the cause of consciousness as there is opposition between them. Two things which in their natures are opposed to each other cannot be related as cause and effect, or there can be no causal relationship between them. If matter is to give birth to consciousness it has to cease to be matter because as matter it cannot be the cause of consciousness. And in giving birth to consciousness if matter ceases to be matter we will have no means to prove or establish that matter is the cause of consciousness. On the other hand, if we think that matter is somehow the cause of consciousness then nothing can prevent us from relating causally any two things, or causation will then have no meaning. To say that two things are causally related is meaningful only when there is something common between the cause and effect, but not otherwise. The same arguments hold good against the belief that consciousness and matter can somehow be related or co-exist.

Another characteristic of matter is that it is always an object of knowledge to consciousness. And if consciousness is to be a manifestation of matter it should have a form, and be an object of knowledge. Though matter as such is not an object of perception all its manifestations are objects of perceptual knowledge. Can we say that it is also the case with consciousness? Is consciousness an object of knowledge? Can there be knowledge of consciousness as we can have knowledge of the various forms of matter? Can we perceive consciousness as we can perceive material objects? In this context, it may be pointed out that matter as such is also not an object of perception, as what we perceive are the forms of its manifestation. Matter as such may not have any specific quality, but all the qualities that belong to its manifestations belong to it in a sense. Similarly, can we say that though consciousness as such is not an object of knowledge it can still be known through its manifestations or functions? But we face a basic problem here. Though matter as such is not an object of knowledge yet we come to know matter in and through the forms of its manifestation. All the forms of matter have some content, and are known in terms of their qualities or attributes. There can be no knowledge of a thing which has no qualities or attributes as to have knowledge of a thing is to be able to say something about the thing. The knowledge of an object must have some content. Moreover, the senses can perceive objects in terms of their qualities or attributes. And a thing which has no qualities cannot be perceived or known as to know is to know something about a thing. Now, in what sense we can say that consciousness is an object of knowledge? If we understand consciousness as that which is present or is revealed in and through all the cognitive acts, like knowing, or as that because of which we know, understand, think, etc. we have to admit the involvement of two things in all cognitive acts. One is that because of which we see or perceive or know, and the other is that by means of which we see or perceive or know. Even though the ability to know, or the consciousness is present, if one does not have certain sense organs one cannot perceive certain qualities of a thing. Sense organs are as essential as consciousness to perceive or know things, and both are not the same. Similarly the mind is involved in the functions like thinking and remembering. Thinking, understanding, remembering, etc. are the functions of mind as seeing, hearing, etc. are the functions of sense organs, and consciousness knows things with the help of these cognitive instruments. And knowing a thing is not the same as being aware of a thing as in knowing a thing we know something about the thing which we can describe and communicate. The sense organs, as instruments of cognition, cannot by themselves perceive objects if they are not inspired by consciousness. In other words, seeing is different from hearing though both are functions of cognition, and we come to know different qualities of things by means of sense organs. The functions are different because of the involvement of different sense organs. Seeing is the function of the eyes, and hearing the function of ears, but in both consciousness is present. Thus seeing, hearing, etc. involve the functions of different sense organs in addition to consciousness. Similarly consciousness is present in all the functions of mind. But we cannot say that consciousness depends upon such functions to reveal or manifest itself. It reveals itself without depending upon any instruments of cognition. On the other hand, if we say that consciousness reveals or manifests itself it may mean that consciousness has the option not to reveal or manifest itself, whereas consciousness reveals or manifests itself by its very nature or presence. Consciousness reveals itself by its very presence, or its presence is its revelation because consciousness cannot be otherwise. It is present in man even when he is not doing anything. For instance, when man is not seeing or knowing or understanding we cannot say that consciousness is not present in him. Consciousness, which is the very being or essence of man, does not depend for its existence or revelation on anything else though we may adduce such functions as seeing, thinking, etc. as proof for its existence, if its existence requires proof at all. Man may need or depend on proof to know the existence of things other than himself, but not to know himself. He may also offer proof for his existence to others, such as he is talking or doing something, to show that he is, but does not need any proof for himself as in trying to do so his existence is proved or presupposed. Similarly, consciousness which is involved in knowing, thinking, understanding, proving, or in all the functions of the mind and senses does not depend upon those functions for its knowledge as they depend upon it to know or understand things. Consciousness is self-revealing, or it is its own revelation because of its very nature. However, as we come to know consciousness through such functions like perceiving, knowing, etc. we construe that in the absence of such functions consciousness is also absent. Light is required to illuminate objects but it does not require another light to illuminate itself as it is self-illuminating.

The object of the above discussion is to show that consciousness cannot be an object of knowledge. It also does not depend upon its manifestations for its knowledge as the so-called manifestations of consciousness in which the various instruments of knowledge are involved are not really the manifestations of consciousness. However, consciousness as such or in itself, and the consciousness that is known through its involvement in all the cognitive acts are one and the same. But at the level of empirical experience consciousness is known as that because of which we know things, whereas its knowledge by being is never absent. Moreover, in the case of consciousness there is no difference between the consciousness that is known in and through the functions like knowing, thinking, etc. and the consciousness that is self-revealing. The difference is in the way it is known. We cannot think of a consciousness to which the consciousness involved in all the cognitive acts is an object. However, the difference is significant in the sense that though consciousness is known by its very presence or existence is nevertheless viewed wrongly as an object of proof or requiring proof. Therefore to think that we know consciousness is meaningless as it amounts to saying that fire burns itself. We know fire when it burns something, and therefore, we cannot say that fire burns itself when there is no object to burn. Burning is the nature of fire.

If consciousness is not a manifestation of matter as it does not share any of the characteristics of matter, can we think of any kind of relationship between matter and consciousness? If consciousness does not depend upon matter for its existence, or matter cannot be the explanation of consciousness, then matter cannot be the explanation of the world. At the same time, consciousness does not seem to exist by itself as we cannot find disembodied consciousness. Though conceptually matter and consciousness cannot be related as they are opposed to each other in their natures we find in our empirical experience consciousness and matter existing together in all living beings, and more specifically in all human beings. If they cannot exist together because of the opposition between them how to explain their co-existence in man? Man is both matter and spirit or consciousness. Though consciousness is the inner reality of man it is not influenced or affected by the body and its changes. It is the mind which, according to Indian philosophy, is different from consciousness that is affected or influenced by the conditions of human body. As mind and its functions are objects of knowledge to consciousness, just as the senses and their functions, it cannot be confused with consciousness. Mind also belongs to the realm of objects. Mind is internal to man while the world of objects is external to him, but both are objects of knowledge to consciousness. Therefore human body and mind act upon each other and influence each other. Mind is regarded as an internal organ, or the subtle body of man. Consciousness, on the other hand, is not affected by body and its conditions or changes. It knows all without being in any way affected by them.

In view of the fact that there is development in our understanding of matter, can we say that our knowledge or understanding of matter and its nature is perfect and final? Can we say that the final word about matter is uttered either by science or by philosophy? Seeing the development in our understanding of matter can we say that matter as it is known empirically is objectively real? Although matter as it is known empirically is not objectively real we cannot deny validity to empirical experience as it is an experience. But we come to realize the limitations of our empirical experience in knowing the world. And our knowledge of matter as it is mediated to us through the instruments of cognition cannot be perfect or completely objective. We cannot see the most subtle things with our sense organs, and yet we cannot deny validity to our sense experience. It is only in relation to or in the light of scientific knowledge we doubt the objective validity of our empirical knowledge, but not otherwise. Now, we can ask whether our ordinary knowledge of things or the scientific knowledge of them is true or objective. It is only in relation to scientific knowledge of matter our ordinary knowledge of it is not objective or true, but not otherwise. It is through science we come to know the real or true nature of things we all experience, but the science has not reached the end or final point in our knowledge or understanding of the world. Its knowledge or understanding of the world is not absolute. Our knowledge about the world may undergo change, and till the final word is said by science on the nature of matter we cannot say that we know the true nature of matter. But science has its own limitations in understanding things in view of the methods it adopts, and it is an altogether different matter whether a philosophical understanding of the world should be preferred to scientific understanding of it. However, scientific understanding of matter or the world cannot be wholesome or comprehensive because of its own prejudices.

Can we therefore think that the nature of matter as it is known empirically is not its true or real nature, or the nature of matter as we ordinarily understand it is not objectively real? In other words, there is no reality corresponding to the ordinary understanding of matter, or the reality that is empirically known as the world is not objectively real. Although it is not objectively or ultimately real it is empirically real as without it human life is not possible and meaningful. And if matter which is considered to be the ultimate cause of the world is known to be unreal ultimately all the theories constructed to explain the existence of the world in terms of matter prove to be matters of imagination. When we come to know that the empirical knowledge or understanding of matter has no objective validity we cannot maintain that matter as it is known empirically is the explanation of the world. As our empirical understanding of matter is not valid objectively so is our empirical understanding of the world. There is no matter ultimately or objectively corresponding to our empirical knowledge or understanding of it. How can a reality which does not exist objectively be an object of experience? This we shall discuss in a separate chapter.[4]

If matter as it is known empirically is not real in the ultimate analysis the problem of its relation to consciousness ceases to be relevant. Instead, we have to consider whether matter in its true nature is not really different from consciousness. Now, if the reality which we empirically know or understand as matter is not ultimately or objectively real we have to consider whether the consciousness as we know it at the empirical level is really different or not from the reality which we experience as matter at the empirical level. What appears as matter to empirical experience may not be really different from consciousness as the consciousness which we know or understand at the empirical level may not be its true nature. When we know that the nature of matter as we know it empirically is not its true nature we can also doubt whether the nature of consciousness as we know it empirically is its true or real nature. Therefore the opposition between matter and consciousness which seems to be real at the empirical level may not be real ultimately. They may not be really opposed to each other as both of them may not be really different. This is a possibility which we cannot straightaway deny. Thus as long as we do not know the true nature of a thing we cannot decide whether it can exist by itself or not. Our assertion that matter as we experience it empirically is caused because it is a composite reality or consists of parts is true at the empirical level. But when our empirical understanding of matter is proved to be

4. This is a problem faced even by the scientists. The matter as it is known to empirical experience is known differently by a scientist without there being any change in matter. The same matter or reality is known differently by a scientist and a layman. Why or how *Brahman* is known or seen as world by us is a problem, and the fact that there can be no rationally intelligible answer to the problem is indicated by a highly enigmatic concept of *māyā* in Advaita.

wrong ultimately there is no point in discussing whether matter is the cause of the world of empirical experience. If matter in the sense in which we know and understand it at the empirical level is not real it cannot be the cause of the world. More importantly, the world as a manifestation of matter is equally not real objectively or ultimately. It is a different thing whether matter in its real nature can also be a caused reality or not.

Thus in knowing the true nature of what we experience empirically many problems which our empirical knowledge or understanding of the world gives rise to get themselves dissolved. However, one significant problem as to the nature of relationship between the true nature of what we experience empirically and the reality of our empirical experience remains. Whether the matter in its true nature is the cause of the matter as it is experienced empirically is a different problem which we discuss in a separate chapter. The world of empirical experience is viewed as dependent upon some other reality because such understanding is governed or guided by the laws, especially the law of causation, which are valid within the world of empirical experience. Certain relations and laws are valid and meaningful in the world of empirical experience which may not be valid absolutely as the reality of the empirical experience is itself not real in absolute terms. For instance, we think that matter is the source of energy, but in reality they are not two different things because when the matter is converted into energy that particular amount of matter which is converted into energy is not still there to be related to the energy. And similarly matter is seen as a composite reality, and is therefore seen as caused by coming together of its parts. But matter in the ultimate analysis is not a reality that is composed of parts.

If consciousness cannot be a form of manifestation of matter it cannot also be the true or real nature of matter. The essence of a reality shows itself in and through the manifestations of reality, and if consciousness is the essence of matter it should show itself in all the manifestations of matter, which is not, however, the case. Conceptually also consciousness cannot be the essence of matter, as it amounts to saying that matter is consciousness or consciousness is matter. Can we say that consciousness appears as matter to our empirical knowledge and experience without there being any change in the nature of consciousness? However, to think that consciousness is the true or real nature of matter is not the same as to say that matter is only an appearance of consciousness. If consciousness cannot be a modification or manifestation of matter since consciousness does not share any of the characteristics of matter it cannot be the essence or true or real nature of matter also.

If we think that somehow consciousness appears as matter to our empirical knowledge, as matter appears solid to our senses then we have to explain the origin of the idea of matter which corresponds to our empirical experience of it. In a perceptual illusion one thing appears as some other thing only when there is some similarity between the two which is not, however, the case between matter and spirit. How can anyone mistake consciousness as matter when there is no similarity of any sort between them. If matter is not an illusion as it is an object of perceptual experience universally, we have to think of some other explanation as to why it is known differently in empirical experience. Here we can think of two different positions or two different views about matter, one offered by science or physics and the other given to our ordinary knowledge. Our ordinary knowledge of matter is something different from that of scientific knowledge of matter. Supposing that both the ideas of matter are equally valid because both are based on experience, and refer to something that is there what could then be the possible relationship between the scientific concept of matter and the ordinary or popular concept of it. The problem of relationship between the two views or ideas arises as they are about the same reality. The same reality is seen or known differently. The scientific knowledge of the matter is different from its ordinary knowledge though in reality they are about the same reality. Is the difference in understanding due to our limitations of understanding it, or is it due to change in the nature of the reality? Of course, we do not or rather cannot have two different experiences about the same reality at the same time. Even a scientist who knows matter as a scientist, knows it differently when he sees it with his senses. Here we are not talking about holding different views but two different ways of understanding the same reality which are, however, based on experience. Different people can hold different views or opinions about the same reality at different times, but not at the same time. One cannot hold at the same time two different views about the same reality. When we find conflict between the scientific knowledge or understanding of matter and the ordinary understanding of it though we may give credence to scientific understanding of matter, we have no valid reason to deny validity to our ordinary understanding or knowledge of it. We have to explain then the possibility of ordinary knowledge of matter. These problems will engage our attention later. How do we know that the present-day scientific knowledge of matter is the final word on matter? Do we have any valid reason to believe that science has said the last word about the nature of matter? Science is still growing, and we do not know what more discoveries are possible with regard to matter. But one thing is clear keeping in view the progress science has achieved in understanding matter. The true or real nature of matter is different from the nature of matter as we empirically know or understand. Our knowledge of it though is useful for our practical life is not the real or true knowledge of it. Maybe we come to know that it is not really different from consciousness. Maybe what we know as matter is in reality not different from consciousness, and the reason for knowing so may not be due to any change in the nature of consciousness, but due to perfection in our knowledge. However, we discuss these problems in the last chapter.

5

Consciousness

In trying to understand the nature of *Brahman*, the explanation for the existence of the world of empirical experience, man is guided by his empirical experience, in the sense that he searches for an analogy or a paradigm in the world of empirical experience to understand *Brahman* and its nature. However, in understanding the nature of *Brahman* if we take into consideration the physical world only, the object of empirical experience, our approach to *Brahman* would be significantly different from our approach in which human reality is also taken into consideration and given due importance. If we assume that the reality of man is not different from the reality of the world we are justified in trying to understand the nature of *Brahman* on the basis of our understanding of the world of empirical experience. But as we have shown in the previous chapter the reality of man cannot be explained in terms of matter which is, however, sufficient to understand and explain the physical side or aspect of human reality. Now, if the physical world, the object of man's empirical experience and knowledge, is taken as the starting point of enquiry into the nature of *Brahman*, and the enquiry is guided by our understanding of the physical world and its laws, our understanding of the nature of *Brahman* will be significantly different from the one in which the starting point of enquiry into the nature of *Brahman* is human reality. Why should we accept human reality as our starting point in trying to understand the nature of *Brahman*? What justification do we have in starting our enquiry into the nature of *Brahman* with human reality? Do we have any advantage in accepting human reality as the best possible analogy in understanding the nature of *Brahman*? There are so many things or phenomena in the world of empirical experience which can provide a basis for understanding the nature of *Brahman*, the explanation of the world. However, there are a few things or phenomena which are really helpful in understanding the world of empirical experience. While the process of interaction among the various phenomena of nature give rise to the physical world with all its diversity, the process of evolution gives birth to several forms of life which in a sense culminates in the emergence of man. In addition to the above processes, we find in the reality of man the free flow of creativity because of which certain finer things come into being. Human creativity is the reason or explanation for the existence of much of the world we experience. The different cultures, civilizations, religions, philosophy, literature, music, etc. are the creations of human creativity, and these also help us in understanding the world and its true nature, as the human creativity and its creations add a significant dimension to the world of empirical experience. Even if we consider human creativity as something subjective — for it is not to be found equally in all human beings — still its value in understanding the world cannot be denied as man is an integral part of the world. For instance, the beauty of a flower is also significant in understanding the reality of a tree as its trunk and roots. We cannot say that the beauty of the flower is not significant in understanding the reality of the tree as its trunk and other parts which are more tangible or objective. The human creativity and its creations are as much integral to the world of empirical experience as the mountains and rivers, and help us in knowing or understanding the world as anything else. However, what they reveal about the world the other facts of the world do not reveal though both are integral to the world.

Let us try to understand another significant problem in this connection. Why should we take into consideration the facts of the world in trying to understand the world and its nature? What is that we want to know about the world from the facts, or what is that which the various facts of the world can reveal about the world? Is it the case that every fact, besides revealing itself, can also reveal something about the nature of the world? On the other hand, if the facts cannot reveal the nature of the world our study of facts will have no significance in understanding the world. However, the facts can reveal something about the world as they integrally belong to the world, and therefore share the reality of the world though the world as such is not a fact among other facts. And in trying to understand the world we are not trying to understand a reality which is completely different from or other than the facts of empirical experience. The world as such has no existence so that it can be observed, studied and explained independently of the facts of empirical experience. The world exists or lives in the facts, and reveals itself and its nature in and through the facts. The facts constitute the world as we mean by world the unity of the facts, or if there is unity among the facts that unity is what we mean by world. What kind of unity we can think of the world? Is it like the unity of a room or box? A box in a way forms the unity of the things it contains or a room is the unity of the things that are within it. We can think of several kinds of unity. Clay is the unity of all the things made of clay, a tree is the unity of all its parts, like branches and leaves. A human being is the unity of the limbs as well as his creations. All the intellectual creations of man have their unity in his creativity. A tree is one or a unity of its parts as the same life sap pervades all the parts of the tree. Human creativity is the source as well as the unity of his varied creations. The sap of a tree, its life, runs through all its parts, and sustains their growth. A substance is the unity of all the things that are made of it, and is present in all of them. Since the world as such is not a fact, but exists in the facts, to know the world is to know that which is the reality of the facts, or that which is essentially present in all the facts. Therefore in trying to know and understand the world we are not trying to know something over and above the facts of empirical experience, but to know or understand the reality that is present in all the facts, or is the essence of the facts. Essence is what sustains a thing, and gives it an identity, or is that in terms of which a thing is identified and defined. Without its essence a thing cannot exist as it is the reality of the thing. All other things that belong to a thing are not essential for its existence and identity. Although we do not have direct access to the essence of a thing, yet we try to understand it in terms of that which sustains it. In other words, what is co-eternal with a thing or without which the thing cannot be known and identified is usually known as the essence of that thing or the self of it. In a way a thing is known by its essence. Though people differ in identifying the essence of a thing yet they agree that the essence means the essential reality of a thing, or is the real or true nature of the thing. Essential nature of a thing can also be called the nature of a thing as nature is what is essential to a thing, and a thing is known in terms of its nature. The essential nature of a thing remains changeless while other qualities of the thing may change, and even be destroyed, like its form. It is a different problem as to the nature of relationship between essence and other qualities of a thing. While some of the qualities or attributes of a thing are contingent, the essence of a thing is co-eternal with the thing. We cannot find a thing without its essence as the essence is that which sustains the thing, and gives it its identity. At the same time, we cannot identify a thing or reality with its essence, as a thing can have certain qualities or attributes which it acquires, and are therefore not essential to it. But all the things or all the phenomena of nature may not have the same thing as their essence. The essence of fire is not the same as that of water. The essence of earth is different from that of other things. The essence of man is not the same as the essence of other living beings.

Now, can we think of one and the same reality as the essence of all that is there, or common to all the things and phenomena we experience? In other words, is it possible to think of a reality which is present in all that is there in the world, and is therefore known as the reality as well as the unity of the world? The problem of searching for the essence of all that is there would be legitimate and significant if we can understand and explain what we mean by essence in the case of the world as we can understand and explain the essence of earth or water. The fact that each thing or phenomenon we experience in the world has its essence does not mean that they all have a common essence. Can we think of something which all the essences have in common except the term or name? If we define essence as what is changeless in a thing or a phenomenon then all the things in the world have something in common. What is unchanging in everything is what is common to everything. Though this seems to be a formal definition of essence it is a definition of essence. Instead of trying to know whether the things of the world have something in common we can ask the question whether they are sustained by the same reality. We know what sustains all the material objects is matter, or the reality that is commonly present in all the material things is matter, as they cannot exist without matter. We may therefore say that matter is the reality or the essence of all the physical objects, as what is essential to matter is found in all the material objects. A material thing or object is that which can be perceived or known or enjoyed, or anything that is an object of knowledge or experience or enjoyment is matter, or the various forms of its manifestation. The defining characteristic of matter, according to Indian philosophy, is its being an object of knowledge or experience or enjoyment. It is the Indian way of defining matter which is the same as the modern conception of matter as what occupies space or what has extension. What has no form, and therefore does not occupy space, is not an object of knowledge (cognition) or experience.

As pointed out earlier anything that is an object of knowledge or experience or enjoyment is matter, or the different forms of its manifestation. Matter manifests itself in different forms, and we know that they are the forms of matter as they have matter as their reality. To say that matter constitutes the reality of all the physical things in the world is to say that without matter they cannot exist. Matter is the explanation of their existence as well as their unity. To say, on the other hand, that matter is the substance of all that is physical is to assume that matter has a uniform nature, and is so present in all the physical things, which is not, however, the case. It is meaningful to think of gold as the substance of all that is made of gold, or clay as the substance of all that is made of clay as we can identify gold or clay in all the things made of gold or clay. But that is not the case with all the material or physical objects. Matter has no clear or specific identity like gold or clay. Earth, water, fire, air, plants and trees and the bodies of all living beings are manifestations of matter. Therefore, when we say that much of the world or the whole world with the exception of spirit or consciousness is material or physical it does not mean that the objects of the world are alike in every respect, or are manifestations of the same substance called matter as we do not know what matter is. Hard rocks, flowing rivers, burning fire, moving air, shining light, etc. are all seen as manifestations of matter though at the level of empirical experience we do not find anything that is common to them. However, we consider them all as forms of matter or the forms of its manifestation. We cannot, therefore, define matter known in its varied forms of manifestation, in similar or identical terms. However, some philosophers define matter in terms of atoms or as atomic in its structure. But to say that matter is atomic in structure is not to say anything meaningful about the reality or nature of matter. It only means that matter is analysable, or it has parts. All that is material or physical is analysable into its ultimate constituents. But what is the nature of those ultimate constituents of matter is something that is still a mystery as what is the real or true nature of those ultimate particles of matter is not known definitely. We discuss this problem in another chapter.

However, the point we are trying to make is that matter is not a substance with a uniform nature as we do not see any one substance constituting the reality of things which are physical or material. Therefore, we can think of matter as an idea, or at the most it refers to a reality which is the essence of all that is physical. And to say that matter is the essence of all that is physical is not to say anything significant about the nature of matter. As the essence of all the physical or material things of the world matter is not something that can be directly observed. There is no pure matter, or matter as such which is not the essence of any physical thing or phenomenon. Matter is known as the reality or essence of what is physical in the world of empirical experience, and as the essence of various physical things or phenomena it differs from phenomenon to phenomenon.

However, in relation to spirit or consciousness matter is known or is identified as that which is the object of knowledge or experience or enjoyment. The most basic categories of empirical experience are knower and known or subject and object as in the absence of either of them empirical experience is not possible. While consciousness is known as the knower or subject, matter is known as the object. Matter is an object that can be observed, known, studied and understood, and the reality that knows or experiences matter is different from matter. As the knower or observer or analyser of matter consciousness is other than and different from matter. Consciousness to which matter is always given as an object of knowledge or experience or understanding is opposed to matter in nature, and because of the opposition between them one cannot be the manifestation of the other, or one cannot be the explanation of the other. As an object of knowledge and enjoyment matter cannot have anything in common with consciousness. We can only say that both are real. What is then the nature of matter? We may try to understand the nature of matter by finding out what is common to all that is physical or material. Our understanding of matter as that which is an object of knowledge or experience or enjoyment is in a sense an attempt to define matter in formal terms, but not to say anything about its nature or essence. Different physical things or phenomena have different characteristics or qualities which are not, however, common to all the physical things. To say that matter is that which occupies space and is affected by time does not say anything about the nature of matter. Some philosophers are of the view that consciousness or spirit also occupies space as it is found invariably in a human body, and therefore has the same extension as that of a body. There is no disembodied spirit or disembodied consciousness.

In the Indian philosophical tradition even those who are avowedly materialists, like Cārvākas, and other realist philosophers like Nyāya and Vaiśeṣika, did not try to understand the nature of matter. They understand it as that which is an object of sense-experience, and atomic in structure. As pointed out earlier, in saying that matter is atomic they mean that matter is analysable. It is not homogeneous and un-analysable like *Brahman* of the Vedānta. Beyond that they have not tried to understand what really matter is. Now, we have to point out that the scientific understanding of matter is different from that of philosophers and common people. However, philosophers are not equipped to know the ultimate or real nature of matter as their understanding of matter is purely conceptual though based on empirical experience. They try to understand its nature purely in terms of the analysis of the concept of matter and other related problems. Conceptual analysis of matter is valuable as in understanding matter we have to first understand what we mean by matter or how do we define it. As the physicists depend on a particular manifestation of matter their understanding of matter cannot be as comprehensive as that of a philosopher who takes into consideration all the forms of manifestation of matter which includes man and his mind. As the physical aspect of human reality is a manifestation of matter man can know better the nature of matter as he knows it directly. Human body and mind are physical, and they cannot be experimented upon in a laboratory as any other manifestation of matter. Human body is living matter, if we can use the expression, when compared to matter outside the human body, and in knowing the nature of matter we cannot exclude human body and mind, especially the creative aspect of human mind and its varied creations.

Thus a deeper understanding of the nature of matter can help us in understanding the problem of consciousness, and its relation to matter. Human reality in which both matter and spirit or consciousness are present or are in a sense integrated can be our starting point in trying to understand the nature of matter as well as of consciousness. Human reality provides us a better analogy to understand the nature of matter as well as its relation to spirit. However, we find in human reality a conflict between matter and spirit as well as harmony between them. The conflict between matter or human body and spirit is more acute in man whether it is encouraged by religious or spiritual traditions or not. We also find in the reality of man the harmony between them, and that provides a better analogy in understanding the nature of matter as well as its relation to spirit. Man is both matter and spirit, or body and self, and according to popular understanding these are two basically different realities, somehow living together in man. But as man attaches different values to spirit and matter in which the matter is looked down upon as an obstacle or hindrance to know the nature of spirit, and even as an enemy to spirit, it becomes difficult to have a dispassionate understanding of man as a unity of matter and spirit. However, for the purpose of analysis and understanding we use the categories of matter and spirit, and accept their independence in trying to understand them and their relationship.

We find two different approaches to the problem of relationship between matter and spirit. According to one approach, matter is primordial, and it is the only reality which is ultimately real, and consciousness depends for its existence on matter. The spirit or consciousness cannot exist by itself as we do not find pure or disembodied spirit as we can find pure matter. Pure spirit or pure consciousness in the sense unmixed with matter or not depending upon matter for its existence and manifestation is a myth, whereas pure matter is real. Even in man consciousness is not completely independent of human body and mind. This is clearly evident in the cases of swoon and stupor in which consciousness is clearly known to depend upon human body and its proper or healthy functioning. Moreover, the bodily states affect or influence the spirit, and in the absence of a body the spirit also ceases to exist. And we do not have evidence to prove the existence of spirit without a body. According to this view, spirit has only a functional value and existence. It is known to exist because certain functions, like cognition, require its presence.

According to the other approach spirit is primordial, and it is the ultimate reality. The matter as we know it empirically is only an illusion as it does not really exist. Although we do not know the existence of pure or disembodied spirit yet it is the spirit which dominates matter and controls it. It is the spirit which is the glory of man, and hence that of the whole creation. Even God is conceived as pure spirit, and without spirit everything is darkness in the sense there will be no light of knowledge. The matter cannot know itself. To use the analogy of Sāṁkhya, while the matter is blind, the spirit is lame or un-dynamic.[1] Therefore the coming together of the two marks the beginning of the process of evolution, the reason for the existence of the world of our empirical experience. Thus the world as we know it is neither pure matter nor pure spirit as its existence is due to the interplay between matter and spirit. However, it is the spirit that dominates the world, and guides it. Even if we are not prepared to accept the dominance of the spirit in the development of the world we have to admit that the spirit, being immanent in the world, helps the

1. *Sāṁkhya Kārikā*, v. 21.

orderly development of the world. We have to admit also that much of the world as we know it is the creation of man in whom both matter and spirit find their unity. But how far the reality of man can help us in understanding the true nature of matter or spirit. Human reality has one advantage in knowing the true nature of matter or spirit as man can know his reality directly and immediately. Man's knowledge of things other than himself is indirect or inferential, and his knowledge of matter is based on his observation of matter in its manifestations. But man can know matter directly in its manifestation as his body, which includes his mind. However, he cannot know what sustains the world and unites it, or the essence of the world as he can know his true or real nature or his essence. His knowledge of the essence or true nature of the world is indirect or inferential. In other words, what man can know directly are the discrete facts of the world, but not the reality that sustains them and unites them as well. More importantly, man can know or understand the nature of relationship between matter and consciousness, or his body and spirit, by knowing himself. As he is both matter and spirit he can know the nature of both directly and immediately.

However, man's understanding of the relationship between body and spirit can be influenced by his existential concerns, and therefore it may be difficult for him to be really objective in understanding himself. His existential concerns and his religious beliefs can influence his understanding of himself as well as his understanding of the relationship between body and spirit. He can be influenced by his religious beliefs to think that his body is the source of his finiteness and imperfection, and is an obstacle or hindrance to realize his self which is immortal and perfect. The body is the source of all evil and suffering, and therefore the self is to be freed from the influence of the body. Such an attitude may impair one's sense of objectivity in understanding the nature of matter. Man is influenced by the idea that the body is perishable as it is liable to change, and cannot therefore be the source of his real happiness and perfection, whereas the self is immortal and perfect though corrupted by its association with the body.

According to the other view of man, spirit has no independent existence. It is viewed as an epiphenomenon or a by-product of matter in its manifestation as human body. This view of man also impairs his sense of objectivity in understanding the nature of matter or his body, and its relation to consciousness. Thus by attaching certain values either to his body or to his spirit man fails to be objective in his understanding the nature of consciousness or of matter. However, in trying to understand the nature of one the other need not be despised as the objective of understanding one is linked to the objective of understanding the other. An objective and dispassionate understanding of matter, taking into consideration all the forms of its manifestation, may lead us to think that it is not in the ultimate analysis different from spirit, as our understanding of spirit may equally lead us to the view that spirit cannot be found without its manifestation which is what matter is in its true nature. Is it possible for man to be really objective in understanding matter as long as he is under the influence of his body which is also matter? Can we, on the other hand, say that man's understanding of his body helps him in understanding the real or true nature of matter? Our understanding of matter is mostly based on our observation of material or physical objects. We come into contact with matter in the form of various material objects, and our relation to them depends upon their utility to us. Accordingly we attach values to matter. We seldom take ourselves or the reality of man into consideration in trying to understand the nature of matter. We forget the fact that matter constitutes the reality of man also, because most of the cultures are biased against the physical aspect of man. Materialism, meaning sensual form of human life, impedes in understanding matter in an objective way. In a way our attitude towards our physical nature, instead of helping us in knowing the nature of matter objectively encourages us to develop a negative attitude towards matter, which impairs our objectivity in understanding it. However, we may point out that man's understanding of matter, whether it is philosophical or scientific, is based on his understanding of matter as he observes it outside of himself, as he seldom turns his attention to his own body and mind in understanding the nature of matter directly. It is possible that we can know directly the essential reality or essence of matter in understanding ourselves. This is because the body and mind are manifestations of matter in man. As matter is present in man he can know its nature as well as its relation to spirit directly. In knowing ourselves we know our bodies also as man's knowledge of himself involves his knowledge or understanding of his body and mind. Man's knowledge of himself is not complete without the knowledge of his body and mind as well as their relation to spirit. In what sense do we know our bodies? We know our bodies though not in the manner in which we know an object existing outside of ourselves. Here we have to note a basic difference between our knowledge of our bodies, and the knowledge of a scientist or a physician of a human body. In what way our knowledge of our bodies is different from a physician's knowledge of a human body? We normally do not know our bodies in the sense a physician knows them. Can we therefore say that we do not have knowledge about ourselves which includes knowledge of our bodies? But are we conscious of ourselves as a unity of body and spirit when we know ourselves. Can one say that his sense of his body is like his sense of his dress? Do I ever get the feeling that my body contains me as my house or room contains me? When I say I know something, including my body, am I conscious of myself as a body or as a self-living in a body or is it simply knowing which has no reference to body at all. What is the basis or justification for thinking that we are contained in our bodies, or the spirit or consciousness lives in a body, or is enclosed or entrapped by a body? For instance, sitting in a room I can know the world outside through a window, but my being in a room and looking at the world through a window will have no relevance or significance to my knowledge of the world. It does not matter whether I sit in a room or stand outside the room in observing or knowing the world. They do not affect my knowledge of the world or make any difference in knowing the world. Is this the case with body also? Can one extend the analogy to understand his relation to his body? But this is an absurd problem as I do not know what is it to know without a body. I am never without a body in sensing, perceiving, knowing and understanding. When I cannot know what is it to know without a body it is really meaningless to think that my body is not involved in cognitive acts. Non-involvement of body in all that I know and do is something which I have no means to prove or establish, because I cannot think or understand without the involvement of my body. The problem acquires significance only if I can know things without the involvement of my body which is never the case. Then what does it mean to say that the spirit lives in a body or consciousness is embodied. It is possible to understand this problem meaningfully if we can show or prove the existence of self or spirit or consciousness which is not within a body or a disembodied consciousness or spirit. I can know myself as dressed because I can know what it is to be without a robe or dress, but I cannot think of myself without a body.

We can approach the problem of relationship between the body and consciousness in a different way. The argument for the independent existence of consciousness or spirit is that while the body undergoes change the spirit or consciousness does not change. In other words, the states of body do not affect or influence the state of consciousness. To put it in a slightly intelligible manner we can say that the meaning of body undergoes change, but the meaning of "I" which refers to consciousness does not change, and therefore the meaning of body is not the same as the meaning of "I". The "I" does not refer either to the body or to the mind as they undergo change, while the meaning of "I" remains changeless. Let us try to understand the meaning of "I". If "I" refers to self or consciousness which is changeless then the term "I" should always mean the same, which is not however the case. Can we say the illusion that the meaning of "I" does not undergo any change arises basically because it has no referent? However, the meaning of "I" changes according to the context of its usage, and therefore its meaning is not fixed. All the people use the word "I" but it gets its meaning in terms of the person who uses it, and in terms of the context of its usage in the case of the same person. If one tries to understand the use of the personal pronoun "I" one gets its meaning in terms of the context of its usage. One may here say that the meaning of "I" gets confused because of the association of self with the body and mind. It is perfectly meaningful when I try to describe myself in terms of my body or mind, as for instance, when I say that I am tall. On the other hand, if we think that the term "I" has a meaning which is not to be confused with the context of its usage in which there is reference to body or mind then we have to understand whether it has a meaning independently of the context of its usage. Does it have a content which it can convey when it is used? Words have meaning as they refer to some fact or object which we can know independently of their usage. Can we therefore say that the word "I" has a meaning independently of the context of its usage like any other word ? If that is not the case then we have to admit that its meaning depends upon the context of its usage. That amounts to saying that the term "I" has no content, or it does not refer to anything specifically. If it has a meaning independently of its usage, or the context of its usage then the simple utterance of "I" should mean something, which is not, however, the case. At the most, when someone utters the word "I" it may function like the word "look," that is, to attract or draw attention. Thus it gives rise to the illusion that it refers to something which remains changeless amidst changing body and mind. Moreover, consciousness as such is not an object of knowledge. It has no specific characteristic which can be said in language. To say that consciousness means to be aware of does not mean anything, as consciousness, insofar as our empirical experience is concerned, is meaningful only in relation to something other than itself, as to know or to be aware of is meaningful only in relation to some object.

We now consider another argument or justification in favour of independent existence or reality of consciousness. Consciousness is an independent reality because it does not depend for its existence on any other reality as there is opposition between itself and things other than itself such as matter. To understand the problem at the level of human reality, we find opposition between consciousness and body or the subject and object as one is always a subject and the other is always an object. The subject cannot become an object, and the object a subject. Consciousness is always a subject or knower and matter is always an object of knowledge. One cannot become the other because of the opposition between them, and for the same reason one cannot be the explanation of the other or one cannot be reduced to the other. One is a subject and the other an object, and a subject cannot become an object and an object a subject. In self-consciousness in which the self seems to become an object to itself, what happens is that some idea or image of self becomes an object to consciousness, and the idea or image of self is not completely spiritual as it is always mixed up with what is not spirit. The consciousness to which the idea or image of self becomes an object in self-consciousness never ceases to be consciousness even for a while. Thus what one thinks of himself or his self, in which the idea of body, including mind, is invariably involved is the object of consciousness in the state of self-consciousness. Ideas are also objects of consciousness as they are objects of understanding, and consciousness is involved in understanding also. And because of the opposition the self and body cannot also be related in any manner. But we know that they are related in man as he is a unity of spirit and body. Although we think that man is a unity of both body and spirit a deeper analysis shows that they cannot co-exist or be integrated because of the opposition between them.

If the spirit and body cannot be related or united as we think it is so in the case of human beings we have to explain why they seem to be related. How to understand and explain the unity between matter and spirit which we experience in human reality? Instead of trying to understand the relationship that does not exist between matter and spirit we may have to think whether they are really different. Is it the case that what we think, based on our empirical experience, of matter is not ultimately valid? What is the metaphysical or rational justification for accepting the duality of matter and spirit? The real problem in knowing or understanding the nature of matter and its relation to spirit is to accept the evidence of empirical experience as final or absolute. At the level of empirical experience the duality and opposition between matter and spirit or body and consciousness is real, but how can we say that what is real at the level of empirical experience is ultimately real?

However, we seldom try to understand whether the duality of spirit and matter which we take for granted, or is presupposed in understanding the problem of matter and spirit and their relationship is ultimately real. We have to understand the problem of duality of matter and spirit before we try to understand the nature of relationship between them. We have to give up the idea of duality of matter and spirit as in that case it is not possible to explain their coming together or being related in the reality of man because of the opposition between them. If there is opposition between matter and spirit or body and consciousness how can we explain their unity in the reality of man. On the other hand, if we think that duality is not real in the case of human reality we have to understand the reality of man either in terms of pure matter or pure spirit. But empirically speaking man is a unity of matter and spirit or body and consciousness, and our understanding of human reality in terms of both matter and spirit is both valid and meaningful. If matter and spirit can find their unity in the reality of man how to explain the opposition between them? If matter and spirit cannot be related in any positive manner then we cannot understand the reality of man in whom matter and spirit are related or united. In terms of empirical experience, and the understanding based on it man is neither spirit nor body. And even if we think that matter alone is sufficient to understand and explain the reality of man we cannot equate a rock with man or man with a rock though both of them are forms of matter. There is something in human reality which is not to be found in other material things. We cannot say that man is a purely physical reality like a rock, nor can we say that a rock or any other physical reality has consciousness as their essence. The distinction between physical and spiritual is clear as far as our empirical knowledge or experience is concerned, and therefore we have no justification of any kind in trying to equate them, or explain away the reality of one or the other. In understanding the world of empirical experience, or for that matter even in understanding the nature of matter, human reality plays a crucial role. The scientific understanding of matter does not face certain problems which a philosophical understanding faces as the latter takes into serious consideration the reality of man in understanding the reality of the world. The scientific understanding of the world is based primarily on what can be observed by the senses. It does not take into serious consideration, in understanding the world or the nature of matter, the reality or the being of the scientist who tries to understand the world and matter.

Human reality can play a significant role in understanding the world, including matter, as human reality represents both matter and spirit as in him both are united or are one. And man can know and understand himself or his reality, that is, both body and mind as well as their relation directly or without any mediation. The nature of matter as it manifests in man is significantly different from its nature as manifested in the world of objects. This fact is significant in understanding the reality of matter. Man can know what constitutes his essence or his true reality directly, whereas his knowledge and understanding of what constitutes the essence of the world of objects is indirect. In the case of the world man has to depend upon the manifestation of matter in diverse forms to know or understand the reality or essence of matter, whereas man can know himself or his essence in and through all his manifestations as well as by being the reality underlying the manifestations. He knows himself not only by making himself an object of his observation and knowledge but also by being himself. I know myself not because I can prove my existence, but by being myself as I am basically a conscious being. My existence is self-evident in the sense that I never try to know whether I exist, and I do not depend upon any proof or evidence to know my existence as I do in the case of a reality other than myself.

How do we know that human reality is the best possible analogy to understand the world and its nature? How can we justify the claim that human reality is the key to understand the reality of the world? The reason why man can not only distinguish himself from the world, but can detach or disassociate himself from the world in knowing or understanding the world, is the presence of spirit in him. But man thinks that the spirit within him does not really belong to the world of empirical experience, and therefore does not help him in knowing or understanding the world. And similarly he thinks that his understanding of the world does not help him in understanding himself or his reality, that is, his self. The dichotomy between himself and the world makes man think that the spirit and matter are two different and independent realities. While his body or the physical side of his being belongs to the world of empirical experience, his spirit does not belong to it. Therefore the world cannot be the explanation of the spirit, that is his real being. This basic presupposition about himself influences his understanding of himself as well as his understanding of the world. Such duality or dichotomy also is the reason for giving different values to both matter and spirit.

However, there are views about man in which the duality is

questioned. They try to understand the reality of man either in terms of matter or of spirit. According to some, matter is the only reality that is ultimately real, and it is sufficient to explain the reality of man, including the spirit. But some of the philosophers are of the view that the ultimate reality is spirit and matter as it is known empirically is an illusion. However, some of the philosophers conceive ultimate reality as a personal being, and in his person both matter and spirit are integrated as they form his body and self. Each school of thought has tried its best to justify its position. However, these views though seem to be extreme avoid the problem of relationship between matter and spirit or body and consciousness. If we accept that spirit is the real explanation of man then we have to explain the existence of matter which is empirically as real as consciousness, or if we accept matter as the ultimate explanation of human reality we have to explain the emergence of spirit or consciousness in terms of matter. And attempts are made to explain that matter which is real as far as empirical experience is concerned is not really matter, and is therefore not really different from spirit or consciousness. Is rational or philosophical understanding of the problem adequate to explain the problem, but that is the only way open to us as we cannot think of direct evidence to decide this or that way. However, rational or critical understanding of human reality or of oneself may be meaningful in understanding the problem to a significant extent as ultimately man has to depend upon certain facts in understanding the totality of what is there, and according to this approach human reality is a most significant fact in understanding the world, and therefore a clear and deeper analysis and understanding of human reality or of oneself is more valuable in understanding the problem.

6

Self or Spirit

MATTER as it is known empirically cannot be the explanation for the existence of the world as it is not ultimately real, or the matter as we know it empirically is real only in relation to our empirical experience. However, from the point of view of empirical experience both matter and consciousness are equally real, and as they are opposed to each other one cannot be the explanation of the other. Therefore, in trying to understand the nature of what is ultimately real if we limit ourselves to what we know and understand empirically we have to admit the reality of both matter and spirit. But when we try to understand the nature of matter, taking into consideration all the forms of its manifestation, including the physical side of human reality, as well as the scientific knowledge or understanding of it, we realize that what we know about matter empirically is not its real or true nature. Thus when we realize that matter as we know it empirically is not ultimately real we start doubting the validity of our empirical experience, and the understanding based on it. Therefore our understanding of the world based on empirical experience of it cannot be the sole basis or ground for us to know or understand the nature and meaning of what is ultimately real.

The object of our discussion on consciousness in an earlier chapter was to understand whether consciousness could be the explanation for the existence of the world. We tried therein to make a distinction between consciousness and self or spirit, the essential reality of man. Consciousness is regarded as a defining characteristic of *Brahman*, and at the empirical level, or in relation to the world of empirical experience *Brahman* is known as the essence as well as the unity of all that is there. Therefore consciousness cannot be identified with the self or essence (*ātman*) of man. As the essence of all that is there, consciousness is the essence or self of man also, and therefore the self of man is a clear and direct source of revelation of consciousness to man. Therefore the self of man cannot be identified with *Brahman*, though it is the direct source of revelation of *Brahman* to man. Man, a self-conscious being, comes to know clearly and directly the nature of *Brahman* within himself, or in his self. Even though a direct source of *Brahman*'s revelation to man, the self is always known in its relation to human body and mind, or it is not known independently of a living human being. In the classical Indian tradition of Vedānta, a distinction is made between *Brahman* in itself, and the *Brahman* as enunciated and discussed in the Vedānta texts.[1] In other words, the distinction is between *Brahman* in itself, and the *Brahman* that is known in relation to the world of empirical experience. *Brahman* in itself is a logically valid idea based on man's understanding of the world, but not a reality that can be known either in terms of rational understanding of man or on the authority of the Vedānta texts. On the other hand, as the explanation for the existence of the world, or as what is ultimately real *Brahman* is conceived and defined in relation to the world of empirical experience, and therefore its meaning and validity are in relation to the world of empirical experience, but not independently of it. Therefore, there

1. *Brahman* that is known through the Upaniṣads or as it is understood or conceived by us gets itself conditioned by various factors like language, limitations of human understanding as well as the existential concerns of man. Thus when we find several conceptions of *Brahman* we have to understand that they are different attempts to understand and represent *Brahman* in itself. *Brahman* in itself is known directly by being *Brahman*, in which the distinction between the knower and known is transcended, whereas what we know about *Brahman* through the Upaniṣads is only an indirect way of knowing *Brahman* which is affected or influenced or conditioned by the limitations of the knower.

can be several conceptions of *Brahman* depending upon one's understanding of the world as well as his understanding of himself. The main or major concern of all such conceptions of *Brahman* is their significance to man as well as their sufficiency to explain the existence of the world. And living in the world of empirical experience we cannot judge the validity of the different conceptions of *Brahman* as one cannot be totally objective in understanding their validity. However, it is within the power of man to understand that the different conceptions of *Brahman* cannot be completely objective though subjectively meaningful or significant. Such realization is the reason or the ground to think of *Brahman* in itself of which all the conceptions of *Brahman* are attempts to represent.

All the systems or schools of Vedānta, with the exception of Advaita, tried to understand *Brahman* as the cause of the world, and in understanding the nature or meaning of causation they are guided by the law of causation that operates or manifests in the physical realm of the world. The various examples taken from the world, like the clay and objects made of clay, the sea and the various forms of its modification like the waves, or the seed and the tree in terms of which they tried to understand the causal relation between *Brahman* and the world, fail to explain satisfactorily and consistently the relationship between the world and *Brahman*. We present two of the arguments against the validity of such attempts. Basically, those who have tried to find a causal explanation for the existence of the world have not cared to understand whether the law of causation which is valid within the world of empirical experience or in relation to things of the world can legitimately be applied to the world as a whole which is not a homogeneous reality. World as such is not a thing or an object that exists within space and time. And as our understanding of the world goes on changing because of the continuous development in our knowledge and understanding of the world we cannot think of it as a finite or limited entity. If the world is all that can be known, and is as extensive as space, we cannot think of the world as a finite thing. As space is not finite the world that is co-extensive with space cannot also be finite. And if the world is not finite then there is no scope for another reality to exist which is supposed to be its cause. We cannot imagine the limits of the world as we cannot imagine or think of the limits of space. And as we cannot think of two infinite realities there is no problem of one being the explanation of the other. If *Brahman* is infinite, and the world has no limits, just as space, then only one of them can exist or be real. Since the world is known to all, and as its reality is directly experienced by all it is the only reality that exists. Therefore, instead of trying to know the cause of the world it is meaningful to know or understand the world truly and perfectly. And even if we accept, for the sake of argument, the possibility of a cause for the existence of the world we have to explain the reason for it to create the world whatever may be the mode of causation. And any type of causation is incompatible with the idea of reality that is supposed to be the cause of the world.

How can we know or establish that the world of our empirical experience cannot exist by itself, or is a caused reality? Unless we know clearly that the world is a caused reality we cannot think of a cause of the world, and the only reason why we can think of the world as a caused reality is the fact that the things of the world are composite in nature. They can be analysed into several parts of which they are made. And unless the parts that make up a thing are joined or combined together they cannot come into existence. But there is no argument to prove that the elements which constitute the things of the world are also created as they cannot be analysed any further. They exist by themselves. And unless they combine themselves the things of the world cannot come into existence. Whether an external agency is required to join them, or they combine themselves because of something which is intrinsic to them can be discussed. According to another form of causation, the cause manifests itself into several forms which constitute the world. Now, supposing that the cause of the world exists prior to the existence of the world of forms how to explain the change in the nature of the cause? Unless the cause changes itself the various forms of its manifestation cannot come into existence. And if we think that the reason for the change is inherent in the cause of the world then there can be no beginning to the world. On the other hand, if we think of another reality that produces change in the cause of the world we face the same problem. If the reason for change is inherent in the cause of the world then change is natural, but not caused. Then the cause and effect cannot be differentiated as the process of manifestation is intrinsic to the nature of the cause, or cause cannot be without its manifestation. Therefore, the world process is co-eternal with its cause, and they cannot be different as one cannot be without the other. This basic argument is valid whatever may be the mode or form of causation we attribute to the cause of the world. And if the cause of the world is regarded as matter, as that is the predominant reality of the world of empirical experience, then we face the formidable problem of explaining the reality of consciousness or spirit in terms of matter.

Most of the philosophers of Vedānta tried to understand the relationship between *Brahman* and the world as one of cause and effect, and they tried to understand the nature of causation in terms of analogies mostly taken from the physical world, like the sea and its modifications, or clay and the object made of clay, or seed and tree. However, in the basic texts of Vedānta, the world is seen as a spontaneous and creative expression of *Brahman*. If *Brahman* is fundamentally spiritual then the relationship between *Brahman* and the world should not be understood in terms of causation as found in the physical realm of the world. The world is to *Brahman* as breathing in and breathing out to a living human being, or the creative wisdom (*kāvya*) to a creative person (*kavi*).[2] The world is a creative expression of *Brahman*, and the coming

2. *R̥gveda*, 10.55.5.

into existence of the world from *Brahman* is as spontaneous as the web from a spider, or hair from a living human being, or sparks from a burning fire.[3] Thus if we try to understand the nature of relationship between *Brahman* and the world as seen in the Upaniṣads though conveyed or expressed through highly significant analogies we come to know that there is no relationship in the usual sense between *Brahman* and the world as they are not viewed as two different realities. They are not two. The world is a self-expression of *Brahman*, and *Brahman* being pure spirit cannot be without its self-expression, and the world is a creative expression of *Brahman*. As we cannot separate a person's creativity from himself or the process of breathing from a living person we cannot separate *Brahman* from its creative expression or the world. At the same time, they cannot be identified also as they mean two different things to us at the empirical level. The meaning of the world is not the same as that of *Brahman*, and therefore they cannot be identified as in terms of their meaning they are different. Nevertheless, they refer to the same reality. In other words, the terms world and *Brahman* refer to the same reality though they carry different meanings. Thus Advaita does not mean oneness of the world and *Brahman*, but their non-difference or their not being two. *Brahman* and the world are like the sun and sunshine or a gem and its lustre.[4]

Let us try to understand the reasoning process involved in reaching the conclusion that *Brahman* is the true nature of what we know as the world, and therefore they are not really different. What is the Upaniṣadic way of discovering *Brahman* or how they

3. *Muṇḍaka Upaniṣad*, 1.1.7; *Bṛhadāraṇyaka Upaniṣad*, 2.1.20.

4. What is empirically known as world is in its true nature *Brahman*. Though the world and *Brahman* refer to the same reality, they are not identical. Therefore the assertion that the world is not different from *Brahman* does not mean that the world and *Brahman* are the same, as in terms of their conception they are so different they cannot be identified even by an ordinary person. Nevertheless, they do not refer to two different realities.

have reached the idea of *Brahman*? What are the presuppositions of the Upaniṣads in conceiving *Brahman* as the creative source of the world or the world as a creative expression of *Brahman*? In the Vedānta tradition, the different conceptions of ultimate reality as found in different systems of Indian philosophy are analysed and critically evaluated. The ultimate reality is conceived to explain the world as most of the philosophers think that without understanding the reason for the existence of the world we cannot really understand the world. To understand a thing is to be able to explain its existence. Therefore the validity of a concept of the ultimate reality is its ability or efficiency to explain the existence of the world. As the conception of the reality is based on rational understanding of man its validity depends upon its logical consistency as well as its sufficiency to explain the existence of the world. The reality by whatever term we may know it, is seen as the reason for the existence of the world, or it is the cause of the world. Śaṅkara in his writings tried to understand the logic involved in such conceptions, and by following the same logic tried to show how such conceptions of ultimate reality are not adequate or sufficient to explain the existence of the world. He tried to show the logical fallacies involved in the formation of such conceptions. He even tried to show that the conceptions of ultimate reality based on rational understanding end up in fallacies and contradictions. Though reason is highly significant or helpful in understanding the world, the existence of the world cannot be explained in terms of reason. The basic assumption of most of the systems of metaphysics is that the world cannot exist by itself, or has no independent existence, and therefore the task of metaphysics is to find out the cause of the world, or to find an explanation for the existence of the world. We rarely come across a change in such an attitude of philosophers towards the world. As they assume the dependent existence of the world they think to have an understanding of the world we have to know or understand its cause. Thus a causal explanation of the world is regarded as the main concern of metaphysics. This is based on the belief that causation is valid even outside the world of empirical experience, or before the world has come into existence. Since everything we experience in the world is caused the world also must have a cause, and it is the problem of metaphysics to find it out. In all this they have not tried to know whether they have really understood the world and its nature. They have taken for granted that they know the world and its nature, and therefore the only thing they need to know about the world is the reason for its existence. However, they have not tried to understand whether the world can exist by itself, instead they tried to find a causal explanation for its existence. In other words, before trying to explain the existence of the world they should have tried to know the world objectively and comprehensively.

The attempt to know the world perfectly or objectively is to give up the pre-conceived notion that the world cannot exist by itself. The notion that the world cannot exist by itself is due to the extension of the principle of causation, which is valid within the world of empirical experience, to world itself. The world is the totality or unity of things and phenomena that are known, and those that can be known. To regard the world as one is to see it as the unity of diverse things and phenomena we experience, and that requires justification. And if we think that the world is not a limited reality, though our knowledge of it is limited, we have to understand whether the law of causation is really meaningful in relation to it. If the world is all that is there to think of its explanation in causal terms is really absurd as there can be no other reality which could be considered as its cause or explanation. Therefore, instead of trying to explain the existence of the world, very few of the philosophers of India have turned their attention towards knowing or understanding its true or real nature. According to them, the concern of metaphysics is not to explain the existence of the world, but to know its real or true nature. Before we try to explain the existence of the world we have to understand whether it needs any explanation for its existence. Thus Advaita is not a system of metaphysics in the accepted sense of the term as in it no attempt is made to explain the existence of the world in terms of *Brahman*. The object of Advaita is to know the reality of the world truly or objectively. The world is real as it is an object of experience for all, or our enquiry into its true nature presupposes its existence.

But what reasons are there to think that the world as we experience it empirically is not its real or true nature? How can we say that the world we experience is not really or ultimately real? If it is ultimately real it does not depend for its existence on another reality. In other words, if the world can exist by itself or has an existence of its own then the object of metaphysics is to know its real or true nature as it does not require any explanation for its existence. How can we know whether the world we experience is ultimately real or not? How to make a distinction between real and ultimately real, or what distinguishes real from the ultimately real? Do they refer to two different realities or refer to one and the same reality? If they refer to two different realities in what way they are related? On the other hand, if they refer to the same reality how to make the distinction? We say that a thing is ultimately real when it exists by itself or does not depend upon another reality for its existence. The true nature of a thing or the essence or essential nature of a thing, which is changeless in a thing, can be said to exist by itself, whereas certain characteristics which a thing acquires in course of its existence may change or be destroyed, and they cannot therefore be ultimately real though we cannot deny reality to them. What comes into existence can cease to exist also. A thing is known differently in terms of its changed conditions, whereas it retains its identity in terms of its essence or what does not change. Unless we discuss these we cannot say whether the world of our empirical experience is ultimately real or not. Here again we have to make a distinction between a material reality and a spiritual reality. The manner in which a material thing remains the same, and at the same time undergoes change is different from the manner in which a spiritual reality remains identical despite change. For instance, gold remains the same in all the forms it acquires, or the clay remains the same in all its forms. As gold or clay the thing is changeless, while the forms they acquire change. A golden object is real as long as it lasts whereas gold is real as long as gold exists. To put it differently a golden object is real, and in relation to the golden object gold is ultimately real. Therefore, what is ultimately real is not in a sense different from what is real or what is changing. Gold is ultimately real in relation to the various objects of gold. But gold is also not ultimately real when we view it in relation to the elements that constitute it. The elements that constitute the gold are ultimately real, whereas gold and the objects made of gold are real, or the true nature of golden objects is gold, and the elements are the true nature of gold. Thus when we cannot analyse a thing any further we arrive at the true nature of the thing which is ultimately real because it can exist by itself; it is uncaused. The true nature of a thing is also known as its essence because it sustains the thing, and is the reason for the identity of the thing, and the essence of a thing is not outside the thing. A thing can also be known in terms of its qualities which it acquires, but its identity is due to its essence as the thing is known in terms of its essence. In this sense a thing cannot exist without its essence as the essence of a thing sustains the thing, and gives it its identity. The objects made of clay cannot exist without clay, their essence. The objects may lose their identity as objects, but not their identity as clay which is their essence. Thus the essence or true nature of a thing is what is essential for the existence of a thing, or is intrinsic to it. And essence cannot exist without the thing as it is the true nature of the thing. Therefore the ultimate reality of a thing is not different from the thing. Now, what kind of relation we can think of between the real and the ultimately real? In a sense they are not related as they are not two different things. The two terms, real and ultimately real, refer to the same thing. The true nature or essence of a thing is intrinsic to the thing, and helps in knowing the thing as without knowing the essence of a thing our knowledge of the thing is not complete or perfect. Therefore, when we think in terms of the true nature or essence of a thing we are not trying to create any difference between the thing and its essence or true nature. Can we then say that the reality of a thing is the manifestation of its essence? As the essence of a thing and the thing cannot be separated, as both refer to the same reality, or as one has no meaning independently of the other we cannot say that the real is the manifestation or the appearance of what is ultimately real. On the other hand, to justify the assertion that one is the manifestation of the other we must be able to know or identify the essence independently of its manifestation, which is not, however, the case. We cannot view them as separate as they are not known independently of each other. Why then we make the distinction between real and ultimately real, or what justification is there to distinguish them when they are not different? Before we discuss this problem let us to try to understand the distinction between the two as available in the spiritual realm which also can help us in understanding the problem more clearly. A spiritual reality is known for its creativity and freedom, and we know a spiritual reality through its expressions. Usually we talk of a creative person and his creations, or a thinker and his thoughts, or a musician and his musical creations, or a poet and his creations, and thereby we seem to make a distinction between the creativity of a person and its creations or the forms of its expression. As we distinguish a thinker from his thoughts, or a creative person from his creations we may see them as different, and therefore try to establish a relation between them. They cannot be identified, and at the same time, they cannot be viewed as two different things. We can find a thinker without thinking, or a musician without music though we cannot think of thought or music without the thinker or the musician. Thought as an expression of a thinker is not possible without the thinker though thinker can be seen without thinking. Now, what sort of relation we can think of between the thinker and the thought or the musician and the music? Man is basically a knower, though he does not always know, for instance, when he is in sleep. And we know that knowing is effortless when compared to thinking and singing, as knowing involves less or no effort when compared to thinking and singing. The point we are trying to make is that in all those things there is no causal relationship between the knower and knowledge, and thinker and thinking. We cannot say that the thinker is the cause of thinking or the knower is the cause of knowing.

Creativity finds its expression in various ways, and the various forms of expression of creativity are not related to a creative person in the usual sense of being related. However, the creativity cannot be identified with the forms of expression as creativity is more than the forms of its expression. Creativity transcends its forms as it cannot be identified with any of the forms of its expression, howsoever significant they may be from the point of view of humanity. Thus the creativity and the forms of its expression cannot be identified as the creativity is more than the forms of its expression, and for that reason the forms of expression cannot be regarded as different from creativity. The creativity expresses itself spontaneously and freely which are the characteristics of a spiritual reality. If the spirit is infinite its forms of expression are also infinite as we cannot set limits to the forms of its expression, and the world is an expression of *Brahman* which is spiritual. Therefore *Brahman* and the world are not related in any empirical sense of the term. And at the same time, they cannot be identified as the spirit transcends the forms of its expression. They cannot therefore be regarded as one. They are not different, or are not two, which in no sense means that they are one.

Why then *Brahman* is identified with consciousness by most of the philosophers of Vedānta, and the world is seen as non-spiritual? Here we have to digress a little to understand the Vedic position on this problem. According to the classical or Vedic Indian understanding of the world all that is there (*viśvam*) is classified into three realms of *ādhidaivika*, the realm of the deities or the manifestation of the Divine in and through the phenomena of nature, *ādhibhautika*, the physical realm of the world and *ādhyātmika* or the manifestation of the divine at the human level. The divine or *Brahman* is present in all the three realms though its manifestation is more clear to man in his own reality as he can know his reality directly and immediately. Whether man can see or not the divine is present in all that is there, or all that is there is an abode of the divine. It is not the reality of man alone which is a source of divine revelation, but the entire world if one can see. And the Upaniṣads, the basic texts on Vedānta philosophy, primarily try to understand the nature of the divine or *Brahman* as it reveals itself in the reality of man (*adhyātma*).[5] This should not be taken to mean that *Brahman* is not present in the other two realms of *ādhidaivika* and *ādhibhautika* of the world. Even in the Upaniṣads, the cardinal statements of Vedānta like "I am *Brahman*" or "you are That" and "all is *Brahman*" have the same import though the statements gain their significance in terms of the Upaniṣadic enquiry, and the contexts in which they are made. If the starting point of enquiry is man or human reality the statements that "I am *Brahman*" or "you are That" are significant, and if the starting point of enquiry is the world of empirical experience the statement "all is *Brahman*" is significant. But all the statements are meant to show that *Brahman* is the reality not only of man but of

---

5. According to the classical Indian tradition, the world is classified into three realms: the realm of the deities (*ādhidaivika*), the physical realm of the world (*ādhibhautika*) and the realm of human reality (*adhyātma*). While the Vedic Saṁhitās try to understand the divine in relation to the realm of deities, the Brāhmaṇa texts try to understand the divine in its relation to the material or physical world, and in the Upaniṣads attempts are made to see the presence of the divine in the inner reality of man.

the whole world. All that is there or the world is true (*satyam*) and *Brahman* is the truth of the world (*satyasya satyam*).[6] In our language the world is real, but *Brahman* is ultimately real, or *Brahman* is the self or essence of the world. If we keep this statement in view we can understand the problem of world-*Brahman* relation, as the other Upaniṣadic statements help in understanding the problem of man-*Brahman* relation. Therefore, whether the starting point of metaphysical enquiry is man or the world the conclusion tends to be the same that *Brahman* is the essence or reality of man as well as the essence or reality of the world. In other words, *Brahman* is the essence of all that is there, including man. Thus the world and man have *Brahman* as their essence or self, or *Brahman* is ultimately real while the world is real.

In the Upaniṣads, the term *ātman* is used not only in relation to man, but also in relation to the world. After showing how *Brahman* is the essence of all that is there, it is said that the same essence is the essence (*ātman*) of man also "you are That" (essence).[7] *Brahman* is first known as the essence of all that is there before it is known as the essence of man. On the other hand, if *Brahman* is the essence of man only then there would be no logical ground or justification to reach the conclusion that *Brahman* is the essence of all that is there or the world. In all the examples or analogies chosen in the *Chāndogya Upaniṣad* in teaching or explaining that *Brahman* is the essence (*ātman*) of all that is there, and therefore the essence (*ātman*) of man also, the purpose is to show that *Brahman* is the self or essence of all that is there, and without it the world cannot sustain itself.[8] *Brahman* is all, or is the essential reality of all that is there. The same conclusion can be reached by starting the enquiry with the reality of man. The essence (*ātman*) of man is spirit or self, and that is the revelation of *Brahman* in

---

6. *Bṛhadāraṇyaka Upaniṇad*, 2.1.20.
7. *Chāndogya Upaniṣad*, 6.9 and 6.10.
8. *Chāndogya Upaniṣad*, 6.12-13.

man, or *Brahman* which is the essence of all is known as the spirit or self in man. And man knows *Brahman*, the essence of all that is there, directly within himself as his self or consciousness.

In the world of empirical experience, *Brahman* is known as the self or essence of all that is there. It is the essence or self of each and every phenomenon of nature. Being the essence or self of everything, *Brahman* is present in all that is there. Therefore, *Brahman* is not a reality different from the reality of man or of the world. The world is real, and *Brahman* is the essence of that reality. The world is real, and *Brahman* is what is ultimately real in the world. And the most significant thing to be noted in this connection is that the idea of *Brahman* is meaningless without its being the essence of the world as the reality of *Brahman* can be conceived only in relation to the world of empirical experience. It is only by forming an abstract idea of what is essential to the world we may arrive at the notion of *Brahman* in itself which is valid only logically. We cannot think of *Brahman* without its creativity or self-expression which is the world, and therefore the world cannot have its existence without *Brahman* whose self-expression it is. Thus *Brahman* and world are not two realities, and are not therefore different. At the same time, the meaning of the world is not the same as that of *Brahman* though they do not refer to two different realities. The world though is not different from *Brahman* is not the same as *Brahman*; it is not identical with *Brahman*. As the creative expression of *Brahman* the world is logically dependent upon *Brahman* for its existence, but *Brahman* does not depend upon the world for its existence, though *Brahman* is known in relation to the world. *Brahman* transcends the forms of its expression or the world, and as *Brahman* is spiritual it cannot be determined or exhausted in terms of the forms of its expression. Nevertheless, it is present in all the forms of its expression as their essence or *ātman*. Thus the world and *Brahman* though refer to the same reality are, however, different in terms of their significance to man. Therefore, if we can realize that what we know as world is in reality or in its true nature is *Brahman*, Advaita is realized. *Brahman* is the essence (*ātman*) of all that is there, including man, and therefore *Brahman* will have no meaning to man independently of the world, and world can have no existence independently of *Brahman*. That makes all the difference between an ordinary man, and a man with the knowledge of *Brahman*.

Bibliography

Bṛhadāraṇyaka Upaniṣad, tr. Swami Madhavananda, Mayavati, Almora: Advaita Ashrama, 1950.

Chāndogya Upaniṣad, tr. Swami Gambhirananda, Calcutta: Advaita Ashrama, 1983.

Indian Philosophy, S. Radhakrishnan, 2 vols., London: George Allen & Unwin Ltd., 1956.

Muṇḍaka Upaniṣad, tr. Swami Gambhirananda, Calcutta: Advaita Ashrama, 1957.

Ṛgveda Saṁhitā with Sayana Bhāṣya, 5 vols., Poona: Vaidika Samshodhana Mandala, 1978.

Sāṁkha Kārikā, Isvara Krishna, ed. and tr. S.S. Suryanarayana Sastri, University of Madras, 1973.

Index